TRACING ANCESTORS
AMONG THE
FIVE CIVILIZED TRIBES

TRACING ANCESTORS
AMONG THE
FIVE CIVILIZED
TRIBES

SOUTHEASTERN INDIANS
PRIOR TO REMOVAL

RACHAL MILLS LENNON
CERTIFIED GENEALOGICAL
RECORDS SPECIALIST

Genealogical Publishing Company
Baltimore, Maryland
2002

Published by Genealogical Publishing Co., Inc.
Baltimore, Maryland
Second printing, 2002
Third printing, 2003
Fourth printing, 2005
Library of Congress Catalogue Card Number 2001099390
International Standard Book Number 0-8063-1688-8
Made in the United States of America

TABLE OF CONTENTS

TABLE OF ILLUSTRATIONS

FIGURES

TO MY LEGENDARY CHOCTAW PRINCESS

and my Grandmother

who always believed in her

INTRODUCTION

The history and culture of the American South are unique, owing chiefly to the intermingling of the races and the diverse ethnic backgrounds of countless families. Modern Southerners proudly boast traditions—real or not—of Native American ancestry. Odds are, these traditions lead directly back to the so-called Five Civilized Tribes. The Chickasaw, Cherokee, Choctaw, Creek, and Seminole Indians dominated a broad swath of territory from North Carolina to Mississippi before their forced removal westward. Long hailed for their adaptability to "white" ways (hence the designation "civilized"), these nations have gained near honorific status among Southeastern genealogists.

Because mixed ancestry is so common among Southern families, it is not always easy to isolate and identify a particular Indian ancestor. Generally, if the accounts of family elders can be believed, the Native American progenitor lived in the not-too-distant-past: "Grandma's Grandma [or mother, father, or whatever] was a full-blooded Indian. S/he had high cheekbones and coal-black hair to the day s/he died." Despite the strength of such conviction, however, many researchers pursuing these traditions feel they are chasing a will o' the wisp.

In fact, tracing political and social minorities is quite difficult. The struggle between competing cultures led to separation and discrimination among even those with a long history of coexistence. Whether the ensuing discrimination was ethnic or religious, whether it occurred in the Americas or in the Old World, the very fact that power, privilege, and prejudice have been common to all societies creates challenging conditions for genealogists and historians. Traditionally, the underclass has been far less likely to keep records, either because its members were inadequately educated or because record keeping was politically dangerous. At the same time, many individuals escaped the underclass by concealing or even denying their own cultural, ethnic, or religious heritage. Modern researchers therefore struggle to uncover what their forebears struggled to hide.

This work provides the cultural, genealogical, historical, and social context researchers need to turn family stories into proved lineages. It does not pretend to be definitive or exhaustive—no work can be. Rather, it outlines a path through the maze of confusing customs and unique records that typically stymie Native American research; and its master bibliography should provide many new trails to explore along that main path. Numerous resources do exist for finding Indian forebears in the Southeast prior to removal. This handbook should help family historians find both the resources and the forebears.

Rachal Mills Lennon, CGRS

PART ONE

COLONIAL &
EARLY STATE
RECORDS

CHAPTER 1

A RESEARCH FRAMEWORK: CHRONOLOGY, CUSTOMS & HISTORY

D ifficulties in documenting Native American ancestry have two primary causes. First, the search commonly begins with the premise that the Indian connection occurred within "living memory"—or at least within the memory of someone personally known by today's older generations. Second, the search typically focuses on that wonderful, vast, but often irrelevant body of "Indian records" created by the United States government.[1] These are the roadblocks this chapter addresses.

MOVING BEYOND THE STEREOTYPE

The basis for these research problems becomes evident when one applies a chronological framework to the family tradition. Some 150–180 years have passed since the various removals of Southeastern Indians to points west of the Mississippi. Therefore, if the grandmother who related the family tradition was born a hundred or so years ago, her own grandmother would have been born about the time of the removal—or even a generation after. By extension, one of the following research situations would exist:[2]

1. The Indian forebear should be on one or more of the federal, removal-era rolls, if living at the time of the tribal relocation; or

2. The Indian forebear should be on one or more of the federal rolls in Indian territory, if born after the relocation; or

3. The Indian forebear should be on one or more of the federal rolls drafted for one of the few Eastern reservations;[3] or

4. The Indian forebear belonged to a family that chose not to remove west with its tribe, accepted a federal grant of land in or near his/her home, and became American citizens; or

5. The Indian forebear belonged to a family that—in order to stay behind—"disappeared" into a remote (often wooded and swampy) environment that white settlers and authorities had scarcely penetrated; or

6. The account of Grandma's Grandma is apocryphal, and the real "full-blood" forebear lived in a considerably more distant time.

Almost without fail, researchers who experience difficulty finding the alleged Indian ancestors report that they have already explored possibilities one through four above with no success. Much of the federal trove of "Indian records" is widely available today.[4] Supplemented by other holdings in tribal archives, they are the subject of most lectures on American Indian research. But when Grandma's Grandma is not found in those records conveniently labelled "Indian," what then?

The first and best rule is this: *one should proceed to research the family in the same manner as if the Indian tradition did not exist*. As the ancestral lines of the presumed Indian are extended back an additional generation or two—or even five or six—a Native American connection (or clues to one) could surface in any type of record. In the research process, the chance of that discovery can be greatly enhanced in two ways. First, one needs to learn the social fabric and political history of the area in which the alleged Indian line resided. Second, research should be expanded to include a wealth of pre-removal records that generally receive short shrift in American genealogy and history.[5]

SOCIAL FABRIC

In at least one regard, the American Southeast differed little from the rest of the hemisphere. Two or more conflicting cultures tried to coexist—at best, to survive; at worst, to eliminate conflict by eliminating each other. Attitudes ingrained in both societies contribute to the challenge of genealogy. Culture shaped the manner in which ethnic groups mixed and blended. It affected the terms by which relationships were identified. And it determined the type and amount of genealogical data recorded.

THE NATURE OF MISCEGENATION

All societies, historically, have believed their own culture to be superior to others. Neither European Americans nor Native Americans were exceptions. However, the political and economic dominance that the Europeans achieved over the natives had genealogically crucial results. Intermarriage between white and red Americans was discouraged by most elements of white society—a sentiment that was sometimes reciprocated. Skin color was a visible badge of the class to which each person belonged. By extension, attaining full rights of citizenship and unhampered economic opportunity in a white-dominated region usually depended upon whether individuals could (or were willing to) hide part of their heritage.

Thus, the researcher who attempts to prove the existence of an Indian forebear must consider the social circumstances under which ancestral families passed through the portals from one race to another.[6]

Mergers into Caucasian Society

Given the prejudices involved, most intermarriages of a full-blood Indian to a Caucasian occurred in an environment in which the white spouse did not have to face the disapproval of white peers. Commonly, this was (1) a frontier with few white families and reasonably peaceful relations; or (2) an Indian village into which the white person was welcomed—usually as a government agent, trader, minister, schoolteacher, or craftsman employed to teach such skills as blacksmithing or weaving. *Therefore, the likeliest place and time in which a researcher will find*

*the union of a full-blood white to a full-blood Indian will be the point at which
a likely ancestor resided in environments 1 or 2.* "Ordinary" research in
"ordinary" sources needs to be conducted until a family member is
placed into one situation or the other.

Contrary to popular assumption, there was no "one-drop rule," under
which the slightest bit of color tainted a family forever. (If there were,
how could so many American families have traditions of nonwhite
forebears?) Offspring of Indian-white couples, if they chose to "marry
white" and live in white society, could experience prejudice or enjoy
acceptance, depending upon other factors.

Without wealth or connections to a prominent family, acceptance
into the dominant white society was more likely to depend upon
whether the multiracial person was "light" or "dark." It could take two or
three successive generations of Indian-white marriage in the tribal
environment before someone of Indian background could live an "ordinary" life in white society—basically: vote or hold office, participate in
the social life of the community, send children to "white" schools, and
see those children freely court "white" sweethearts.

David Moniac Jr., an antebellum sheriff of Baldwin County, Alabama, offers a useful example of the stages of "acceptance" into white
society through which a mixed line might progress. Genetically, David
was four generations removed from one full-blood Creek ancestress,
three from another. David's paternal great-grandfather, a "Hollander" or
"Polander" named Dixon "Dick" Moniac, married the half-blood Polly
Colbert and settled in the Creek Nation. Their son, Captain Samuel
Moniac, was genetically just one-fourth Indian and was described by
white contemporaries as "one of the most intelligent half-breds [sic] in
the Nation." Sam's wife was of similar background—the quarter-blood
Elizabeth Weatherford, sister of the Creek chief William Weatherford
and daughter of the half-blood Sehoy McPherson by the white Charles
Weatherford.[7] A Creek chief, wealthy tavern keeper, and planter, Sam
straddled the margins of both worlds—Indian and white. When the
Creek nation split into factions during the War of 1812 over the issue of
whether white settlers should be accepted or exterminated, Sam aligned
with the pro-white faction. As a result, he suffered heavily under

opposing Creeks in the 1813 massacre of white settlers along Tensaw River.[8]

Sam and Elizabeth's son David (genetically one-quarter Indian) was appointed to West Point Academy from Alabama and was breveted a second-lieutenant in the U.S. Army. Resigning in 1822, he married Mary Powell (exact ethnic composition uncertain; but she was a cousin of the Seminole chief Osceola) and became a cotton planter on ancestral homelands in Baldwin County, Alabama. When the Florida Wars erupted in 1836, David was commissioned by the U.S. Army to lead a Creek company against the Seminoles; he died a major in that conflict. Although considered "Indian," David enjoyed quasi-acceptance by whites, who respected his education, intelligence, and prosperity. By the next generation, the stigma of the family's Indian origins had been effectively shed: David Moniac Jr. was a two-term sheriff of Baldwin County—a post strictly reserved for whites.[9]

Mixed-race individuals of less prominence and wealth followed the same pattern of assimilation but may not be so easily documented. A contrasting example is provided by a cluster of Choctaw families living on the northeastern fringe of tribal territory that is now Tuscaloosa County, Alabama. Wishing to avoid both the removal and white conflict, they burrowed into the wooded swamps along the Sipsey River. With time, whites did encroach, but on a nonthreatening basis since they practiced the same low-profile, self-sufficient lifestyle. Longtime residents of the area report the death of the county's "last Choctaw" in the mid-1900s; but the line did not die out. Descendants of the tribe had for several generations intermarried with the compatible white newcomers, until their Indianness "faded" sufficiently for them to join society's mainstream. Genealogists of these families, pursuing a tradition that Grandma's Grandma was Choctaw, will not find her by searching "Indian" records. They succeed in establishing the Indian connection only by doing "ordinary" research—i.e., taking their lines from the present to the past, generation by generation, until they reach a point at which "color" begins to be mentioned or implied in "ordinary" records.

Obviously, if Grandma's Grandma appears repeatedly as a "white" and "ordinary" wife and mother in everyday records of the American past, the odds of her being full-blood Indian are virtually nil. She was more likely at least two or three generations removed. If Grandma's Grandma was indeed born in the mid-1800s, then the genealogist may need to extend the family line to the early-1800s, to the pre-Revolutionary period, or even to the 1600s, before the full-blood Indian is found. This would particularly be so among the Cherokee.

Once researchers conclude that Grandma's Grandma was, at best, a half-blood or an Indian quadroon (one fourth) or octoroon (one eighth), they commonly assume that the Indian ancestry exists in her *maternal* line. While odds favor Indian female–white male couples, the assumption of one begs trouble. Any number of instances can be documented in which white females married Indian males, usually within an Indian village. The Cherokee censuses of 1825 and 1828 reveal that roughly 30 percent of all mixed marriages within the nation were those in which the wife was white and the husband was Indian. (See figure 1.)

Mergers into Black Society

Many Native Americans of mixed race bore African as well as (or instead of) Caucasian ancestry. Runaway slaves frequently sought refuge

Figure 1

Blacks and Whites within the Cherokee Nation, 1825 and 1828[10]

1825				1828			
BLACK SLAVES*	WHITE HUSBANDS	WHITE WIVES	TOTAL	BLACK SLAVES*	WHITE HUSBANDS[†]	WHITE WIVES[†]	TOTAL
1,277	147	73	15,060	1,238	144	61	14,972

* These censuses enumerate no free blacks or black spouses.
† The reference here is to Indian-white unions, not black-white unions.

in Indian villages. Some were returned by the tribes, some were not. Some were enslaved by the Indians, others were allowed to remain as free, and some of the enslaved ones were ultimately manumitted by their red masters. Other blacks were introduced into the tribes by the Indian traders, some as slaves, some as wives or concubines. Some slaves were blacks taken from "white society" by Indian raiding parties. Manumitted slaves and mulatto children of the traders were frequently absorbed into the tribes, particularly among the Creek and their ethnic kin, the Seminole—Osceola's black wife being a prominent case in point.[11]

Some freedmen migrated west with the tribes; others preferred to stay behind under U.S. authority, and some families who stayed behind ultimately changed their minds. Black Tom, for example, was a freed slave of the Choctaw nation who remained in Greene County, Alabama, after most of the tribe moved west. At his death there in 1830 he left a will, duly processed in Greene, in which he made bequests to his "two wives and their children"—the first wife being the black Sally and the second being the Indian Baspasa. Offspring of both wives eventually moved to Oklahoma, where Sally's line lived as Choctaw even though, genetically, some of the individuals had no Indian strain whatsoever.[12]

Native American mergers into black families, slave and free, also occurred in white settlements. From the earliest days of contact, the Native Americans had two commodities to offer whites in exchange for European merchandise: peltry and Indian slaves taken in battles with (or raids against) other tribes. By the mid-1700s, most whites considered Indian slavery too problematic to be profitable; the diminishing Indian population had reduced the supply, and Indian slaves absconded with too-great frequency—returning to their birth tribes or joining others closer at hand.[13] By the close of the Revolution, white enslavement of Indians was discouraged, if not banned, in most new states.

However, that century and a half of Indian slavery left its mark on the complexion of the African slave population with whom they lived, worked, and socialized. It also left a legacy of public records on black-Indian slaves. In addition to all the records that African-American researchers routinely search, valuable genealogical data can be found in suits for freedom filed—and won—by Southeastern slaves on the basis of descent from a Native American female held in bondage after Indian slavery was abolished.[14]

Black-Indian assimilation also occurred when isolated communities of free blacks or mulattoes merged with remnants of Indian tribes. North Carolina's Lumbees and Virginia's Gingaskins, Nansemonds, and Nottaways illustrate just how deep into colonial history one may have to delve to identify the specific ethnic origins of multiracial families.[15]

Researchers who try to document the ethnicity of specific families face another significant handicap: the ambiguity of records. The numerous errors for which censuses are notorious extend also to the matter of race, and many scribes referred to those with mixed Indian-white ancestry as *half-breed* or *mustee* (an English corruption of the Spanish *mestizo*), regardless of the exact ethnic mixture. Outside a tribe, those of mixed Indian-black ancestry were more likely to carry a *black* or *mulatto* label, unless the Indian component or association was dominant. Some more particular scribes might identify multiracials as *griffe* or *zambo*; but even these terms were used ambiguously by some to signify biracial black-Indian mixtures and by others for people with triracial black, Indian, and white ancestry.

The bottom line is this: *it is essential that researchers locate as many documents as possible which bear on the subject.* After all relevant evidence is gathered, they must carefully consider the nature and quality of each piece of evidence, appraise the degree to which each scribe or informant was knowledgeable or biased about the matter, weigh the data and circumstances against the known patterns that reliable researchers have defined for that class of evidence, then determine where the greater weight of evidence lies. Conflicting evidence is a fact of life for genealogists. Yet researchers must be guided by that same evidence—the basic purpose of genealogy being, of course, to *discover ancestry* rather than to promote preconceived notions.

HANDICAPS CREATED BY INDIAN CULTURE

The Southeastern Indian's concepts of kin, family, and relationships differed in significant ways from concepts within societies of Judeo-

Christian origins. Therein lie the roots of many genealogical problems. Among the most fundamental are ones involving identifications of clans and tribes, terms to describe relationships, and taboos that limit both oral and documentary sources.

Identification by Clan

A major characteristic of the Southeastern Indians was clan membership. Tribes were organized into smaller clans ("families")—Bear, Deer, and Wind clans, to use some Creek examples—which were more important than birth town or other symbols of identity. More than anything else, this clan membership determined social relationships. If a Bear member visited another town, he stayed with and was fed by the Bear clan members of that town. If a Bear member committed a crime or transgression and fled to avoid punishment, another member of his Bear clan had to take the punishment. Vengeance and wars frequently pitted clan against clan, not just tribe against tribe.

Within this clan structure, females were heads and descent was matrilineal—traced through mothers, rather than fathers. No one could take a spouse within his or her own clan, although there was no prohibition against marriage between blood relatives of a different clan. When a couple married, the man became an "honorary" or temporary member of the wife's clan. Their children belonged to the mother's clan, not the father's.[16]

Identification of Tribe

Family relationships extended across not only town lines but also tribal ones. During periods of peace, Indian males appeared frequently in the villages of tribes other than their own. The day books of the Choctaw trading post at Saint Stephens, Mississippi Territory (present South Alabama), for example, are replete with entries for purchases made by non-Choctaws. In just a few months of 1804, as a case in point, one finds Chief Doublehead of the Chickasaw; and Charles Hicks, P. Hildebrand, John Jolly, George Lowrey, John and Samuel Riley, John Rogers, William Shorey, James Vann, John Walker, and U.S. Major

William Lovely of the Cherokee.[17] As early as 1789, the half-Scottish Creek chief, Alexander McGillivray, explained to a treaty commissioner from Virginia that there were various Creeks then living among the Cherokee. "It is a custom of a Creek," McGillivray said, "to disregard all connexions [sic] and country and cleave to his wife; those that have wives abroad never return to their native lands [to live]."[18] Thus, one finds McGillivrays (of several spelling variants) among not only the Creek but the Choctaw and Chickasaw. This intertribal activity was particularly common among the multiracial families—in no small measure because white traders frequently had Indian wives in various towns or villages with which they traded. For example:

Hardy Perry

Petitioning the Council of British West Florida for a grant of land in November 1778, Hardy cited service to the Crown that he had rendered while a resident of the *Choctaw* Nation in Mississippi. Fourteen years later, the commandant of the Natchez District wrote the West Florida governor commending Perry, whom he described as "an American resident established many years in the *Chickasaw* Nation . . . a friend of Payomingo, or Mountain Leader." Perry, the Natchez governor reported, was partial to the Chickasaw Nation "where he has children, grandchildren, and property." As late as 1808, Perry was still active among the Chickasaw. However, he had children, grandchildren, and property amid *both* the Choctaw and the Chickasaw, as evidenced by the numerous records created by and about the Choctaw Perrys during the removals of the 1830s.[19]

Rachel (Durant) Walker Brashears

A quarter-blood Creek, Rachel was born to the marriage of the South Carolina trader, Benjamin (aka Peter) Durant, of Huguenot (and possibly black) extraction, and the half-Creek Sophia McGillivray. As an adult during the War of 1812, Rachel allied with pro-white Creeks in that tribe's "civil war." When, at the close of the war, Rachel's faction petitioned the federal government for reparations, all were identified as

Creek "half-breeds"—including Rachel and her sons, William McGirt and Samuel and Alexander Brashears. Ethnically, the Indian portion of their ancestry was indeed Creek, although all were less than *half* Indian. The Brashear brothers (actually just one-eighth Indian) were born in the *Choctaw* Nation, where their white father was a trader. Rachel and Alexander were still in the Choctaw Nation in 1830, when agent William Ward compiled his list of Choctaws who wished to become Americans rather than migrate to the west. Following the by-then-typical custom of using "half-blood" or "half-breed" for any Indian of mixed ancestry, regardless of exact mixture, the Choctaw agent labelled Rachel a "half-breed woman" and her son "half-blood Creek."[20]

Identification of Individuals

Many genealogists who seek Native American ancestry feel that *names* present their greatest research problem. They point to the phonetic manner in which Indian names were spelled, to the "different naming customs" that Indians followed, and to the fact that many individuals are cited by one name only. All these problems are real enough; and, to the casual researcher, they *can* seem intimidating. Yet these are problems common to genealogical research in most ethnic groups. Phonetic spelling existed everywhere. If *Filecutchy* is recorded as *Phillachache*, is that more intimidating than the appearance of *Lemuel Pyle* as *Samuel Powell?* When more than one *Ahoyo* is found in the Choctaw nation, does that create bigger problems than multiple *John Smiths* in the same white community? When *Hopies-katene* is called *Little Leader*, is it really more confusing than *Cecilius Calvert* being called *Lord Baltimore?*

Yes, Native American names are "different," but using them is no more or less difficult than using names in any society. Multiple individuals of the same name are sorted—regardless of race—by using the principles commonly featured in the case studies in the *National Genealogical Society Quarterly*: a name is only one element by which a researcher identifies any given person. If research is comprehensive and thorough, if one goes beyond the limits of published material to use *all* available records and to extract all relevant clues from the originals, if one views the ancestor as a *whole* individual—a person with specific kin and associates among whom he regularly appears, a person with specific traits and personality and property, a person who lived at a specific landmark at a specific time—and not just a name, then it usually matters little whether the ancestor had one name or two or three. An individual is identifiable by *all* the markers that make him or her unique, not by just a name.

As with research on any ethnic group, genealogists who pursue Native American ancestry must learn the naming patterns characteristic of the society from which descent is suspected. For most major tribes, this can be found in the bulletins and annual reports issued by the Bureau of American Ethnology. These are widely available in the government document sections of major research libraries (primarily university libraries), either in their original hardback form or as part of the microfiched U.S. Serial Set.

Identification of Relationships

By contrast, the genealogical difficulties that *kinship terminology* pose are at once fundamental and monumental. Because of matrilineal descent, Southeastern tribal culture held that a person's most important male relative—the one termed *father*—was the mother's brother, not the biological father. When Southeastern Indians inherited, they traditionally did so from their mother and their mother's brothers, not from their biological fathers. When referring to *sisters* and *brothers*, they might mean uterine siblings *or* the children of their mother's sisters.

Again, these difficulties are typically overcome by learning the customs of a particular tribe and by conducting *thorough, exhaustive* research. The "lists" that are widely available and so appealing to casual researchers will be of little aid with dilemmas of this type. Relationship problems are more often solved by identifying and using *all* relevant materials—daybooks, ledgers, letters, memoirs, travelers' accounts, and all else that places tribal members into the context of everyday life.

Ironically, even though Native-American researchers bemoan the fact that ancestral records are usually "white men's records"—not documents created by Indians themselves—this fact works to their advantage. A deposition by an early Indian, unacculturated to European-American society, might identify a relationship in the Indian manner, while a statement made about him by a white colleague who knew him well is more likely to express the Indian relationship in the European-American terms familiar to us today.

Taboos That Limit Oral Sources

The culture of every society includes taboos. Native Americans were no exception. An example of extreme genealogical significance existed among the Choctaw, for whom it was taboo to speak the name of the dead or for wives to speak the names of their husbands. When John F. H. Claiborne headed a commission to sort out Indian land claims in the early 1840s, he began his labors with lists of tribal members registered under the 1830 Treaty of Dancing Rabbit Creek. The seven thousand Choctaw who preferred to stay in their homeland within Mississippi or Alabama were to be allotted a certain number of acres, according to family size and nature.[21] Claiborne's allotment roll, understandably, had to match the original rolls. However, in the several years that had elapsed between the treaty and the land allotment, a number of the original enrollees had died. When survivors claimed land due to deceased family members, the cultures clashed. Claiborne was duty bound to record the dead enrollees and their relationships to the claimants, but the Choctaw refused to identify their names. Instead, a family would line up and place a stick in a vacant spot to signify the dead one.

Given the Choctaw's lengthy exposure to European-American culture by the 1830s, one might expect some erosion in the taboo. Claiborne noted gradual change among the educated Choctaw, but cited one example of a well-schooled Choctaw in his thirties who could not identify his own mother—not because he felt the taboo should be observed, but because the mother had died when the man was very young and he could not remember anyone referring to her by her name after her death.[22]

POLITICAL HISTORY

Successful searches for people and records are grounded in an understanding of political jurisdictions. This is a particularly complex and confusing matter in the Southeastern United States. On the one hand, researchers must be familiar with the fluctuating geographic bounds of the various Indian nations. On the other hand, they must know the history, territorial limits, and records of not just one but four white nations. England, France, Spain, and the United States all had control over the region.

NATIVE-AMERICAN JURISDICTIONS

Five tribes dominate the records of the American Southeast—the so-called Five Civilized Tribes: Cherokees, Chickasaws, Choctaws, Creeks, and Seminoles. When Native Americans first came into contact with Europeans and Africans, there were dozens of small, autonomous tribes throughout the Southeast; but, by the time of the federal removals, most had disappeared. Some migrated northward and then to the west—notable examples being the Piankashaw and the Sewanee (later Shawnee). Others, decimated by disease or warfare, were absorbed into larger tribes: for example, the Natchez into the Chickasaw and Creek. In the extreme Southeast, many tribes with common cultural roots banded together into the Creek Confederation and the Seminoles.[23]

Figure 2 roughly portrays the elastic bounds of the five major groups, each of whose history is a saga of push, pull, swell, and shrink. Droughts, famines, floods, intertribal warfare, and the encroachment of European settlements continually reshaped the territory that was occupied by any particular Native American group. Prior to the removals, satellite settlements occurred in areas quite removed from the main clusters—a matter of obvious genealogical consequence. While the Chickasaws, for example, generally held to a swath some two hundred

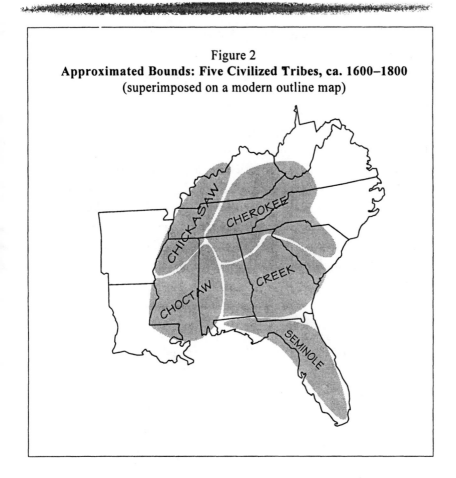

Figure 2
Approximated Bounds: Five Civilized Tribes, ca. 1600–1800
(superimposed on a modern outline map)

or so miles wide, along the eastern bank of the Mississippi River, at least two very distant Chickasaw settlements occurred along the Savannah River that divides South Carolina from Georgia (Augusta area). Similarly, Creek hunters who roamed west of the Mississippi in times of peace moved their families to the Red and Trinity rivers of Oklahoma and Texas even before 1800.[24]

In addition to flexible tribal bounds, genealogists also must bear in mind that town sites also moved or their names were duplicated. The Creek town of Eufaula, for example, stood on the Tallapoosa River in Alabama, at its earliest-known origins. In the 1700s, a new Eufaula was built on the Chattahoochee River below present Columbus, Georgia. In later generations, Creeks from the Chattahoochee-Flint river basin, hunting in Florida, established a third Eufaula near Tampa.

EUROPEAN-AMERICAN JURISDICTIONS

As figure 3 suggests, the American Southeast was a free-form chessboard on which three European nations maneuvered for power. The Indians were their pawns—used to attack, feint, flank, and buffer. Trade goods were the only bribe with which the kings could buy support, and British goods were both better and cheaper. Thus, traders played a paramount role in colonial diplomacy. Genealogists who trace their roots into the colonial Southeast, in search of Indian ancestry, must study not only political bounds but also trade activities that crossed those bounds.

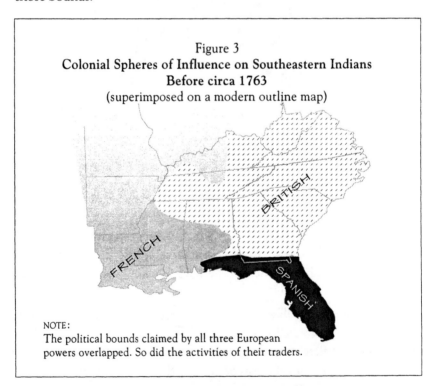

Figure 3
Colonial Spheres of Influence on Southeastern Indians
Before circa 1763
(superimposed on a modern outline map)

NOTE:
The political bounds claimed by all three European
powers overlapped. So did the activities of their traders.

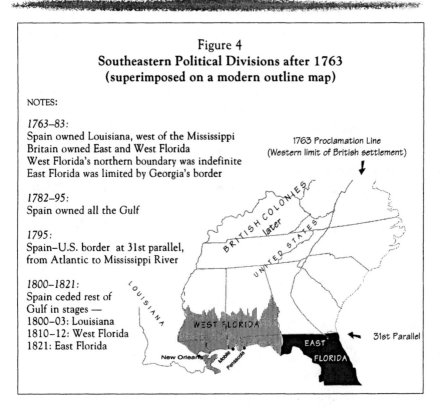

Figure 4
Southeastern Political Divisions after 1763
(superimposed on a modern outline map)

NOTES:

1763–83:
Spain owned Louisiana, west of the Mississippi
Britain owned East and West Florida
West Florida's northern boundary was indefinite
East Florida was limited by Georgia's border

1782–95:
Spain owned all the Gulf

1795:
Spain–U.S. border at 31st parallel,
from Atlantic to Mississippi River

1800–1821:
Spain ceded rest of
Gulf in stages —
1800–03: Louisiana
1810–12: West Florida
1821: East Florida

1763 Proclamation Line
(Western limit of British settlement)

31st Parallel

Together, figures 3 and 4 outline the *governmental* changes that occurred in the Southeast prior to the first federal removals. For the most part, the shifts of dominion followed wins and losses in the French and Indian War (ended 1763), the American Revolution (ended 1783), and the War of 1812 (ended 1815). Because success in genealogical research requires a knowledge of where to go for records (as well as an understanding of why and how the records were created), these political changes are vitally important. If—for example—research or tradition suggests that a family lived "near Mobile" in the later 1700s, at least three options might exist. A family who was there as early as 1780 would be sought in British records. If 1785 were the correct date, the researcher would turn to Spanish papers. If the year were 1796 and the ancestors lived in the Tensas settlement "near Mobile," the ancestors would be within the jurisdiction of the United States. And if one were to believe a piece of misleading information commonly published in research guides—i.e., that Georgia "owned" all lands west of it to the Mississippi—one would almost certainly comb Georgia's records in vain, because that colony and state enjoyed no control at all over the areas it claimed beyond its present bounds.

The government that was in control was not always the one under which a particular trader worked. Prior to 1763, France held the strongest *political* claim to the interior of America—embracing the lands of the Choctaw, Chickasaw, and westernmost Cherokee. Yet, as figure 3 suggests, English *trade* outstripped the French in Cherokee and Chickasaw country. Consequently, amid the French and Indian War, Indian support won Britain a victory—along with which she acquired two Gulf colonies, East and West Florida. (See figure 4.) Although Britain lost the Floridas to Spain during the American Revolution, British traders were not displaced. Spain wisely recognized its inability to compete with English commodities and put British firms in charge of the Indian trade. Consequently, genealogists in search of an Indian trader in the Spanish period would seek primarily Spanish sources; but they would likely find that the trader ancestor was Anglo or Scottish.

CHAPTER 2

COLONIAL RECORDS &
RESEARCH STRATEGIES

The greatest obstacle to pre-removal research has been not a *dearth* of records but the *breadth* of available resources. Vast collections exist in archives of Canada, England, France, Mexico, Scotland, Spain, and the United States—in at least three languages. In the last three decades microfilming projects conducted by several Gulf Coast universities have greatly facilitated access.

The available materials were created from widely differing viewpoints by people with very different objectives. Some record creators were government officials charged with tracking the military might of the tribes and the extent to which they could be used to advance European agendas. Others were businessmen preoccupied with commercial concerns: who was indebted to them, which tribes could furnish the most and best pelts, and how to get cheap trade goods. Still others were churchmen, charged with converting souls and shepherding them to salvation. Finally, many record creators were simply observers, trekking through Indian territories for the adventure and filling their journals and diaries with random encounters and impressions.

TRADE RECORDS

Common images of traders as men of marginal means and questionable character, bumming from village to village, do much injustice to the diversity of this group. Many great American fortunes rest on traffic with the Indians. In the Southeast, the Byrds, Claibornes, Clays, Fleets, and Lees of Virginia; and the Middletons, Moores, Woodwards, and Woolfolks of South Carolina are prime examples.[25] Even genealogists who do not trace back to these elite should not overlook their private papers, typically on deposit in major Southeastern university archives.[26]

For the most part, research in trade-related records will center on two colonial collections: one created by the British colony of South Carolina, the other created by British traders working for the Spanish Crown.

Commissioners on Indian Trade, 1710–65

The first attempts at regulated, large-scale Indian trade apparently date to the South Carolina General Assembly's establishment of the Commission of Indian Trade. Before this, British trade was for the most part conducted on private plantations through Indian hunters and was controlled by the proprietors of those land grants. After 1707, in South Carolina, trade became the domain of powerful Charleston merchants. Traders licensed by the commissioners purchased goods primarily from London and sold them directly to the Indians in the villages or at frontier trading posts. Traders who could not afford to purchase goods hired themselves to the Charleston merchants. Indian *agents*, not to be confused with the traders, were appointed by the government to enforce the commission's rules and regulations out in the field.

The published papers of South Carolina's Commissioners on Indian Trade, 1710–65, are essential for anyone seeking the early roots of mixed-Indian families in the Southeast.[27] Because the commission was in direct conflict and competition with the adjacent French and Spanish colonies, the Commissioners' records have much to say also about trade activities originating at Spanish Saint Augustine or French New Orleans or such French outposts as Chickasaw Bluffs (present Memphis) or Tombigbee in present Alabama.

Genealogical gems are scattered throughout these materials. *In just the first eight years of recorded activity, the journals identify some four hundred whites involved in the industry in one capacity or another*—traders, burdeners (pack men), wagon masters, translators, carpenters, storekeepers, clerks, and military officers. Such numbers give a fair indication of the enormity of the trade and the research potential for genealogists. Indian-white marital or sexual relationships are discussed or implied throughout. For example, on its second day of operation, the board heard a complaint against Philip Gilliard, a trader among the Appalache, who "took a young Indian against her Will for a Wife, and cruelly whipped her and her Brother."[28] In December 1756, the Creek Agent Daniel Pepper wrote the South Carolina governor regarding John Brown, Indian trader at Bread Camp in the Chickasaw nation; he identified Brown as the brother-in-law of Beloved Warrior of the Cherokee town of Tellico.[29] The February 1760 journal of Alexander Miln of Fort Prince George at Keowee among the Lower Creek logged the request of John Winburn for permission to join his family at Tamathlee (a Cherokee town); recorded the death at the fort of "a halfbreed (David McDonald's son)," who had come there with his father amid a smallpox outbreak; and reported news from "Cornelius Ducharty's Woman" at Hiwassee—referring to the Indian wife of Cornelius Doherty, trader among the Cherokee in Tennessee.[30]

Even a cursory scan of the indexes to this set of records makes it obvious why so many Southeastern families claim Indian ancestry. Beyond the basic search for names, the researcher who *reads* the material amassed by this commission will far more clearly understand the mobility of the population, the extensive intercourse between the tribes, and the expanse of the territory a genealogist must search.

Panton, Leslie and Company

At the outbreak of the American Revolution, the British colonies of East and West Florida attracted large numbers of loyalists from Britain's thirteen older colonies. Among these was William Panton, a young Scottish Indian trader from the Charleston firm of John Gordon and Company. By the close of the Revolution, Panton dominated the Florida trade. When Spain won the Floridas, in return for assisting the cause by driving the British from the Gulf, Panton was allowed to remain. Spanish officials realized they could not compete against British-American trade, and Panton recognized the financial opportunity that Spanish allegiance offered. With Spain's approval, his company kept its base in East Florida; but its truckhouses (stores) were scattered as far north as Lookout Mountain, Tennessee, and as far west as the Mississippi River. While other British merchants were similarly retained by the Spanish at New Orleans and Mobile, and still more continued to operate out of the new Atlantic states, Panton soon dominated the Southeastern trade. His firm would continue to do so until well into the nineteenth century. Partners came and went— principally, John Innerarity (Panton's brother-in-law), John Leslie (brother of the Reverend William Leslie, renowned "Father of the Church of Scotland"), Thomas and John Forbes (Scottish nephews of Panton's mentor John Gordon), and Charles McLatchy and William Alexander (both Scottish traders operating in the Southeast before the Revolution)—but, over time, the operation became best known as "Panton, Leslie, and Company."

In the 1970s, historian William S. Coker launched a project to collect all discoverable records created by or relating to Panton, his partners, and their operations. Those papers, assembled from archives in Spain, the British Isles, and the United States, constitute the collection known today as the "Papers of Panton Leslie and Company." The collection is housed at the University of West Florida, Pensacola. Although the collection has been filmed, its size (26 rolls) precludes purchase by most genealogists. Partial or full sets of the film can be found in various university and large city libraries—for example, Samford University Library, Birmingham; the University of Alabama, Tuscaloosa; and the University of Florida, Gainesville.

Before using the collection, genealogists will want to consult two related publications. The first, a historical narrative, treats the Southeastern Indian trade as a whole, with the firm as its focus. The second is a guide and partial index to the collection itself—although *not* an every-name index:

Coker, William S. and Thomas D. Watson. *Indian Traders of the Southeastern Spanish Borderlands: Panton, Leslie & Company and John Forbes & Company, 1783–1847*. Pensacola: University Presses of Florida, 1986.

University of West Florida, comp. *The Papers of Panton, Leslie, and Company*. Woodbridge, Connecticut: Research Publications, 1986.

Within this collection, researchers will find an exceedingly broad array of materials, including (but not limited to) account books; censuses; copies of birth, baptism, and marriage records; correspondence (personal and business); court cases; depositions of whites, Indians, and mixed-bloods; lists of licensed traders; and sales and mortgages of land and personal property.

"GENERAL" GOVERNMENTAL PAPERS

Genealogists are renowned for their use of governmental records housed in local courthouses, town halls, and state archives—as well as post-1782 federal records in the various facilities of the National Archives. Governmental records created on other levels, however, tend to be neglected: i.e., colonial records generated in Europe itself or those sent abroad by colonial governors. The records of the Spanish government are spectacularly rich—those of the French and English somewhat less so—and no quest for elusive Southeastern Indian ancestry could be complete without consulting these resources. While the neglect is usually charged to problems with access and language, neither roadblock is as formidable as assumed. Catalogs, transcripts, and microfilm copies are widely available—so much so that the real limitation is more one of time than access. For those not familiar with French or Spanish, English-language guides can launch a number of extensive searches. Potentially useful documents can often be ordered, for assignment to a translator of choice.

The following collections represent many of the original materials held abroad, for which microfilm copies or transcriptions are available within U.S. repositories.

BRITISH-AMERICAN COLLECTIONS

Library of Congress

In 1898, the Library of Congress embarked upon a project to acquire documents on American history that are housed in archives abroad. The materials it accumulated over the next fifty years include copies from such diverse institutions and agencies as England's Public Record Office (PRO), Bodleian Library, British Museum, Royal Institution, Tower of London, and universities of Oxford and Cambridge; France's Archives des Affairs Étrangères; and Canada's Public Archives in Ottawa—as well as numerous private collections of British noble houses.

Several extensive catalogs (not every-name indexes) have been published and are widely available at major research libraries. Although rich in records relating to Southeastern Indian trade, their value to genealogists transcends ethnic and geographical bounds; all researchers with interests in any of the American colonies should explore the material that is accessible through the following guides:

Anderson, William L., and James A. Lewis. *A Guide to Cherokee Documents in Foreign Archives.* Native American Bibliography Series, no. 4. Metuches, New Jersey: Scarecrow Press, 1983.

————, and Frances G. Davenport. *Guide to the Manuscript Materials for the History of the United States to 1783, in the British Museum, in the Minor London Archives, and in the Libraries of Oxford and Cambridge.* Washington: Carnegie Institution, 1908.

Andrews, Charles M. *Guide to Materials for American History, to 1783, in the Public Record Office of Great Britain.* 2 vols. Washington: Carnegie Institution, 1912–14.

Bell, Herbert C., David W. Parker, et al. *Guide to British West Indian Archive Materials, in London and in the Islands, for the History of the United States.* Washington: Carnegie Institution, 1926.

Griffin, Grace Gardner. *A Guide to Manuscripts Relating to American History in British Depositories, Reproduced from the Division of Manuscripts of the Library of Congress.* Washington: Library of Congress, 1946.

Parker, David W. *Guide to the Materials for United States History in Canadian Archives.* Washington: Carnegie Institution, 1913.

Paullin, Charles O., and Frederic L. Paxson. *Guide to the Materials in London Archives for the History of the United States since 1783.* Washington: Carnegie Institution, 1914.

Lockey Collection

The Lockey Collection of British Records for East Florida, at the P. K. Yonge Library, University of Florida, Gainesville, offers an extensive collection of British materials, focusing upon the region that constitutes modern Florida. A valuable guide is available as

Sturgill, Claude C. *Guide to the British Collection in the P. K. Yonge Library of Florida History.* Gainesville: University of Florida, n.d.

Mississippi Provincial Archives

In 1906, the director of the new Mississippi Department of Archives and History launched a project similar to that underway at the Library of Congress—to copy documents held in British, French, and Spanish archives, relating to the history of Mississippi. Curiously, despite Mississippi's affinity for its British heritage and the comparative ease of copying English-language records, the amount of British-American material actually produced is relatively small. No calendar or catalog is available, but selected documents were published in the following:

Rowland, Dunbar, ed. *Mississippi Provincial Archives, English Dominion.* Nashville: Brandon Printing Co., 1911.

FRENCH-AMERICAN COLLECTIONS

France held dominion over most of the Gulf for longer than any other colonial nation (1699–1763), but it left the least records. Its population was the sparsest; yet the French pattern of colonization in the Southeast was heavily oriented toward Indian trade. Its original colonists were predominantly male, and few of them came to farm. Many were from Canada, where fortunes had already been made in the fur trade. Colonial correspondence from Louisiana (which included the present Southeastern states of Alabama, Arkansas, and Mississippi) is ripe with criticism of the *voyageurs* and *coureurs de bois* (boatmen and woodsmen) who trafficked in hides and bear grease. Both secular and church officials chastised them for the readiness with which they took Indian women to wife or to bed (although trade records leave no doubt that the lifestyle was equally prevalent in British America).

Several collections and publications offer at least a beginning point in research within French archival records.

Louisiana Colonial Records Collection

For the past several decades, the Center for Louisiana Studies at the University of Southwestern Louisiana (USL), Lafayette, has undertaken the microfilming of records relating to the French domain within the present United States. Represented are most relevant materials from the Archives Nationales at Paris and other major French repositories. Although USL has not prepared its own catalog to the one and a half million folios of manuscript material that has been assembled, it has retained the cataloging systems of the original repositories. Thus, researchers can access the USL microfilm through the following French guide:

Astorquia, Madeline Ulane Bonnel, et al. *Guide des sources de l'histoire des États-Unis dans les archives françaises*. Paris: France Expansion, 1976.

The work carries no subject or name indexes. A general reading of the catalog entries is necessary to identify those collections relevant to Indian trade. The text is by no means boring. A general list of the record groups available is found in

Conrad, Glenn R., and Carl A. Brasseaux. *A Selected Bibliography of Scholarly Literature on Colonial Louisiana and New France.* Lafayette: Center for Louisiana Studies, University of Southwestern Louisiana, 1982.

Mississippi Provincial Archives

The French segment of this previously described project produced its largest body of records: thirty-three manuscript volumes relating to the present bounds of Mississippi. Although no general calendar has been marketed for the transcripts that remain housed at the Mississippi Department of Archives and History in Jackson, two published series of selected, translated records make an excellent beginning point:

Rowland, Dunbar, ed., and Albert G. Sanders, translator. *Mississippi Provincial Archives, 1701–1743, French Dominion.* 3 vols. Jackson: Mississippi Department of Archives and History, 1927–32.

———— and Patricia Kay Galloway, ed. *Mississippi Provincial Archives, French Dominion,* vol. 4, *1729–1748;* vol. 5, *1759–63.* Baton Rouge: Louisiana State University Press, ca. 1984.

Vaudreuil Papers

In 1753, the governor of French Louisiana was reassigned to Canada. With him, he carried an immensely important body of records relating to his decade-long administration on the Gulf. Enroute to his new post, his vessel was seized by a British ship; the governor was taken captive, and his archives confiscated. The collection surfaced in 1923, when it was purchased by a nonpublic research institution, the Huntington Library, San Marino, California. While the Huntingdon does not open its holdings for genealogical research, a published calendar of this collection is available; and the library will photocopy documents in response to limited, *academically* oriented requests that cite specific records by document numbers provided in this calendar:

> Barron, Bill. *The Vaudreuil Papers: A Calendar and Index of the Personal and Private Records of Pierre de Regaud de Vaudreuil, Royal Governor of the French Province of Louisiana, 1743–53.* New Orleans: Polyanthos, 1975.

One cannot overemphasize the value of this material for research on French participation in the Southeastern Indian trade, specifically, or Louisiana life and people in general. Accounts, censuses, correspondence, name-specific lists of sundry types, and official orders chronicle a wide variety of activities conducted jointly by the Southeastern tribes and the whites (French and British both) who came among them. In 1743, for example, Vaudreuil's report to France on Indian affairs discusses an attack on the trader William Bienvenu and his wife Mariane, the escape of William, and the capture and later release of Mariane.[31] In 1745, Vaudreuil twice wrote the Alabama commandant about the eleven-year-old son of Pierre Barron of Pointe Coupée; the child had been placed with Talapouches to learn their language.[32] In 1749, the Arkansas commandant submitted a general census of fifty-six named and forty-nine unnamed *voyageurs* in its jurisdiction, together with seven of their *engagés* (contract employees).[33] A 1752 letter from Arkansas reports the arrest of the trader Martin Hurtubise for selling bad liquor to the Indians.[34] A 1743 military list names officers stationed in several Indian tribes.[35]

Miscellaneous

Other materials related to French economic, political, and social commerce with the Southeastern Indians are scattered widely across North America. Researchers will want to examine the following:

> *A Dictionary Catalog of the Edward E. Ayer Collection of Americana and American Indians in the Newberry Library.* 16 vols., 2 supplements. Chicago: Newberry Library, 1961–80.

Beers, Henry Putney. *The French in North America: A Bibliographical Guide to French Archives, Reproductions, and Research Missions.* Baton Rouge: Louisiana State University Press, 1957.

SPANISH-AMERICAN COLLECTIONS

Spain's two regimes in Florida, which spanned three centuries, and its quarter-century in Louisiana produced an array of materials almost beyond the comprehension of those who have not yet used them. Most are, naturally, in the Spanish language. One significant exception is a three-volume series of translated Spanish records produced in 1946:

Kinnaird, Lawrence. *Spain in the Mississippi Valley, 1765–1794,* vols. 2–4 of *Annual Report of the American Historical Association for the Year 1945.* 4 vols. Washington: Government Printing Office, 1946.

Here, researchers will find hundreds of documents from Spanish Archives relating heavily to Anglo-Americans and Indian trade. Lists of Indian towns and their locations (e.g., Creeks, 1793; Choctaws, 1794; etc.) provide handy references to solve the chronic problems of site identification. With both place and personal names, as elsewhere, spelling is phonetic. Spanish scribes did not render sounds in the same manner as English scribes; users should think creatively.

Researchers who are familiar with Spanish (or at least not intimidated by it) will want to continue with study in the following manuscript collections.

Cuban Papers

During the years that Louisiana and the two Floridas belonged to Spain, they were assigned to the vice-royalty of Cuba. When officials of the colony sent reports to their superiors, some copies were directed to Havana, others to Spain itself. When Spain eventually retreated from the New World, much of the Cuban archival material was taken back to Spain, where it became known as the Papeles Procedentes de Cuba (aka Cuban Papers) at the Archivo General de Indias, Seville.

No quest for elusive Southeastern Indian ancestry could be complete without consulting these records; and no single essay could do justice to the vastness of the collection. In general, over a million documents offer censuses, court suits, depositions, land grants, military rosters, oaths of allegiance, petitions, property sales, and virtually every other type of human activity imaginable. At least fifty *legajos* (record groups) treat the Choctaw, a similar number treat the Creek; the Chickasaw and Cherokee are covered in twenty-five or so legajos each. Records of many smaller tribes are scattered throughout. Researchers with Indian interests will find business accounts, correspondences with whites living among the Indians, trader licenses, treaties, and even some tribal censuses (e.g., Alibamon, Apalache, Mobile, and Opelousas, 1774).

Over the past two decades, portions of the Cuban Papers have been microfilmed through the efforts of Tulane University at New Orleans and Louisiana State University (LSU) at Baton Rouge. Partial or full copies of the microfilm are available in various research institutions across the Gulf. Individual reels can be ordered on interlibrary loan through LSU. Most of the documents, logically, are in Spanish, secondarily French, with some in English. However, the following hefty tome offers an English-language index (to subjects and *key individuals*) and descriptions of documents in some two thousand record groups:

> Hill, Roscoe R. *Descriptive Catalogue of the Documents Relating to the History of the United States in the Papeles Procedentes de Cuba, Deposited in the Archivo General de Indias at Seville*. Washington: Carnegie Institution, 1916.

Santo Domingo Papers

A second significant body of Spanish documents relating to the Southeast is the Audiencia de Santo Domingo (aka Santo Domingo Papers). This collection of 140,000 pages relating to the Gulf Coast is drawn from Sección Quinta, Papeles de gobierno de las Secretarías de Despachos y Consejo de Indias (Section 5: Government papers of the Secretaries of Customs [overseas trade] and Councils), of the Archivo

General de Indias. Commonly, genealogists who use the Spanish archival collections are referred first to the Cuban Papers, on the premise that the Santo Domingo Papers are more oriented toward business matters of the colony. That orientation could be considered backward, when one seeks material on individuals engaged in Indian *trade*. Here, one will find appointments of traders and interpreters, complaints by and against traders, and similar documents that help to place specific individuals into place and time within the Indian country.

In the 1960s, Loyola University of New Orleans began an extensive project that organized, calendared, and microfilmed this collection. A copy of the film is available at Loyola and other major research institutions that focus upon Hispanic America. The calendar, which is partially bilingual, has been published as:

De la Peña y Camara, José; Ernest J. Burrus; et al. *Catalogo de documentos del Archivo General de Indias, Sección V, Gobierno, Audiencia de Santo Domingo, sobre la epoca Española de Luisiana.* 2 vols. New Orleans and Madrid: Loyola University, 1968.

Also useful for locating similar and supplementary materials in this same archives is

Bermudez Plata, Cristobal. *El Archivo General de Indias de Sevilla, sede del Americanismo.* Madrid: N.p., 1951.

Fondos de las Floridas

In addition to the foregoing documents, a significant body of papers relating to Spain's control of Louisiana and the Floridas has remained in Cuba. These have been microfilmed (30 rolls) by the L. Kemper Williams Foundation of New Orleans and are housed in the foundation's Historic New Orleans Collection—a research center without equal for Louisiana history. Guides exist as:

Archivo Nacional de Cuba. *Catalogo de los fondos de las Floridas.* Havana: A. Muniz y hermano, 1944.

Cuba. *Documents Pertaining to the Floridas Which Are Kept in Different Archives of Cuba. Appendix No. 1: Official List of Documentary Funds of the Floridas—Now Territories of the States of Louisiana, Alabama, Mississippi, Georgia, and Florida—Kept in the National Archives.* Havana: N.p., 1945.

Mississippi Provincial Archives

The Mississippi project to transcribe foreign documents relating to its early history barely ventured into Spain. While England was viewed as the state's cultural mother and France was a romantic focal point, a comparable level of interest in Spain just failed to ignite. The lapse is ironic, given the fact that most British-American families in colonial Mississippi arrived during the Spanish era, and Spain's records are by far the best of the three colonial powers. Unlike the French and British segments of the project, no publication materialized for the Spanish era. However, the accumulated materials have been filmed for several decades and are available as follows:

Mississippi Writer's Project, Work Projects Administration. *Spanish Provincial Archives, 1759–1806.* Microfilm, 4 rolls. Jackson: Mississippi Department of Archives and History, n.d.

Other Spanish Resources

The Cuban, Fondos, and Santo Domingo papers represent only a fraction of the invaluable Spanish records that genealogists can profitably pursue. Introductions to the others are provided by the following catalogs and guides:

Connor, Jeannette M. *Colonial Records of Spanish Florida; Letters and Reports of Governors and Secular Persons.* Deland: Florida State Historical Society, 1925.

Griffen, William B. *A Calendar of Spanish Records Relating to Florida, 1512–1790.* Saint Augustine: William B. Griffen, 1959.

Guía de fuentes para la historia de Ibero-América conservados en España. Madrid: Dirección General de Archivos y Bibliotecas, 1965, 1969.

Haggard, J. Villasaño. *Handbook for Translators of Spanish Historical Documents.* Austin: University of Texas, 1941.

Holmes, Jack D. L. *Documentos inéditos para la historia de la Luisiana (1792–1810).* Madrid: J. Porrua Turanzas, 1963.

Lockey, Joseph B., comp. *East Florida, 1783–1785: A File of Documents Assembled and Many of Them Translated by Joseph Byrne Lockey.* Berkeley: University of California, 1949.

Paz, Julián. *Catálogo de manuscritos de América existentes en la Biblioteca Nacional.* Madrid: Tip. de Archivos, 1933.

Platt, Lyman D. *Una guía genealógica-histórica de Latinoamerica.* Ramona, California: Acoma Books, 1978.

Robertson, James Alexander. *List of Documents in Spanish Archives Relating to the History of the United States Which Have Been Printed or of Which Transcripts Are Preserved in American Libraries.* Washington: Carnegie Institution, 1910.

Serrano y Sanz, Manuel. *Documentos históricos de la Florida y la Luisiana, siglos XVI y XVIII.* Madrid: Suarez, 1912.

Shepherd, William. *Guide to the Materials for the United States in Spanish Archives (Simancas, the Archivo Histórico Nacional, and Seville).* Washington: Carnegie Institution, 1907.

Steck, Francis B. *A Tentative Guide to Historic Materials on the Spanish Borderlands.* Philadelphia: Catholic Historical Society of Philadelphia, 1943.

Tornero Tinajero, Pablo. *Relaciones de dependencia entre Florida y Estados Unidos, 1783–1820.* Madrid: Ministerio de Asuntos Exteriores, 1979.

Tudela de la Orden, José. *Los manuscritos de América en las Bibliotecas de España.* Madrid: Ediciones Cultura Hispanica, 1954.

AMERICAN COLLECTIONS

A number of U.S. states hold government-related collections valuable to any search for Southeastern Indian ancestry. As with the British, French, and Spanish records, some of the materials were created in the colonies and sent abroad, then replicated for American repositories. Some are historical archives retained in the colonies that subsequently became states, or facsimile collections reconstructed by twentieth-century federal and state libraries.

Florida

Modern Florida is dominated by the Seminoles, descended primarily from a prolonged migration of Lower Creeks and associated tribes into the peninsula. Fierce fighters, they resisted removal longer into the nineteenth century than did the other Southeastern tribes; the last of the Seminole Wars ended in the mid-1850s. Records of the eastern Seminole are not as voluminous, well-known, or used as those of their contemporaries. The major repository for existing materials (aside from the previously discussed Panton, Leslie and Company Papers) is the P. K. Yonge Library, University of Florida, Gainesville. A guide to this library's collections is somewhat out of date, but still valuable:

> *Catalog of the P. K. Yonge Library of Florida History.* 4 vols. Boston: G. K. Hall and Co., 1977.

Researchers will also want to consult

> McCauley, Clay. *The Seminole Indians of Florida,* Smithsonian Institute, Bureau of American Ethnology, Fifth Annual Report, 1883–1884. Washington: Government Printing Office, 1887.

> The Seminole Papers. Florida Historical Society, University of South Florida, Tampa.

Georgia

Georgia's history of Indian-white relations is almost as tumultuous as Florida's—and for far longer. The colony and state created a significant number of records similar to those maintained by and available through the federal government. When used in tandem with the federal records, they add exceptional depth to genealogical research on Indian and mixed-blood families of the Georgia region. Included are such items as claim files, correspondence, letterbooks of traders and factors, licenses to reside among the Cherokee or Creek, and papers of the Brainerd Mission in Northwest Georgia. In addition to these holdings, the Georgia Department of Archives and History in Atlanta maintains an extensive collection of publications and typescripts relating to pre-removal Indians and Indian countrymen (white men living with the Indians), including contemporary memoirs, personal papers, and damage claims generated as a result of Indian-white conflict. As a beginning point for research in these holdings, most researchers use the following manual, which provides little descriptive material but an extensive catalog of available records:

> Davis, Robert Scott. A Guide to Native American (Indian) Research Sources at the Georgia Department of Archives and History. Jasper, Georgia: privately printed, 1985.

North Carolina

North Carolina has been among the most aggressive and the most diligent of the Southeastern states in making its pre-removal Indian records accessible. In the colonial era, the governors and their councils were directly responsible for Indian-white relations. Their activities are extensively documented in a series that has been widely available for many years:

> Saunders, William L., ed. The Colonial Records of North Carolina. 10 vols. Raleigh: P. M. Hale, 1896–90.

Individuals who plan to conduct research onsite at the North Carolina Division of Archives and History in Raleigh should acquire a copy of a second publication:

Spindel, Donna. *Introductory Guide to Indian-Related Records (to 1875) in the North Carolina State Archives*. Raleigh: Division of Archives and History, 1977.

Spindel provides a helpful overview of the various types of resources, a catalog of specific record groups, an inventory of county records that yield a significant amount of material relating to Indians, and a calendar of miscellaneous collections relating to Indians—including London's Public Record Office.

Researchers may also be interested in the Spanish Records Collection of the North Carolina State Archives, which Spindel omits from her Indian guide because the records do not "significantly" deal with North Carolina Indians. (That is not to say that one cannot find material there relating to North Carolina whites who participated in the Indian trade.) The materials stem from another transcription project, this one conducted by North Carolina in the previously discussed Cuban Papers. Two guides are useful:

Manucy, Albert C. "Florida History (1650–1750) in the Spanish Records of North Carolina State Department of Archives and History," *Florida Historical Quarterly* 25 (April 1947): 319–32.

Works Progress Administration, North Carolina. *List of Papeles Procedentes de Cuba (Cuban Papers) in the Archives of the North Carolina Historical Commission*. Raleigh: North Carolina Historic Records Survey, 1942.

Wisconsin

The Lyman C. Draper Manuscripts of the State Historical Society of Wisconsin are regularly used by genealogists interested in the Revolutionary War and the Upper South. However, they deserve far more study by researchers working the Lower South in general and Southeastern Indian connections in particular. Keenly interested in history from his youth, Draper focused his studies on the Revolution and the frontier. As a young man, he crisscrossed the southern and middle states—filling his saddle bags with interview notes and copies of records. Eventually settling into the post of corresponding secretary at the State Historical Society of Wisconsin, he continued his research by mail, penning appeals for manuscripts and recollections. The 492 manuscript volumes he amassed are a unique historical treasure that (in the latest edition) are widely available on 123 reels of microfilm. No master index exists. Several catalogs and one instructive lecture have been published to help researchers identify productive materials.

Hanson, James L. "Born in Virginia . . . Tracking Migration in the Draper Manuscripts." Lecture, annual conference, NGS, Richmond, Virginia, May 1999. Audiocassette tape, Richmond W-4. Hobart, Indiana: Repeat Performance, 1999. For accompanying printed material, see pp. 5–8, *Virginia: Where a Nation Began*, 1999 Conference Syllabus, NGS. Arlington, Virginia: NGS, 1999.

Harper, Josephine L. *Guide to the Draper Manuscripts*. Madison: State Historical Society of Wisconsin, 1983.

The Preston and Virginia Papers of the Draper Collection of Manuscripts, Publications of the State Historical Society of Wisconsin, Calendar Series, vol. 1. Milo M. Quaife, ed. Madison: The Society, 1915.

Calendar of the Kentucky Papers of the Draper Collection of Manuscripts, . . . Calendar Series, vol. 2. Mabel Clare Weakes, ed. Madison: The Society, 1925.

Calendar of the Tennessee and King's Mountain Papers of the Draper Collection of Manuscripts, . . . Calendar Series, vol. 3. Joseph Schafer, superintendent. Madison: The Society, 1929.

Calendar of the George Rogers Clark Papers of the Draper Collection of Manuscripts, . . . Calendar Series, vol. 4. Utica, Kentucky: McDowell Publications, 1985.

Calendar of the Thomas Sumpter Papers of the Draper Collection of Manuscripts, . . . Calendar Series, vol. 5. Utica, Kentucky; McDowell Publications, 1991.

Calendar of the Frontier Wars Papers of the Draper Collection of Manuscripts, . . . Calendar Series, vol. 6. Utica, Kentucky: McDowell Publications, 1991.

The geographic limits expressed or implied by the titles to these guides can be misleading. George Rogers Clark, for example, did not operate in Alabama. Yet the series that carries his name includes information on the pre-1750 Chickasaw adoption of the white James Colbert (trader at the Mussel Shoals in Alabama) and an identification of Colbert's half-Indian children.

Miscellaneous

Beyond the scope of this book exist vast numbers of local church and local government records. Most genealogists are familiar with these holdings or with corresponding guides—at least for the Anglo-American colonies and subsequent states. Researchers are generally less acquainted with the nature and whereabouts of comparable materials produced in the French and Spanish colonies. A useful introduction from a Spanish perspective is provided by

Mills, Elizabeth Shown. "Spanish Records: Locating Anglo and Latin Ancestry in the Colonial Southeast, *National Genealogical Society Quarterly* 73 (December 1985): 243–61.

In this case, the *ethnic* limitations expressed by its title can mislead; the local recordkeeping systems that are described existed in the French regime also. The materials discussed refer to large numbers of Indians (slave and free), multiracials (white and black mixtures), and whites living among the tribes. The Catholic records, which exist for most official posts and a number of missions, offer vital registrations rarely found for minority groups in other early American societies.

For a myriad of more scattered and more obscure resources at archives nationwide, researchers will also want to comb

Chepesiuk, Ron, and Arnold Shankman, *American Indian Archival Material: A Guide to Holdings in the Southeast.* Westport, Connecticut: Greenwood Press, 1982.

Finally, for concise genealogical studies of hundreds of mixed Indian-white-black families, meticulously and extensively researched, see

> Heinegg, Paul. *Free African Americans of North Carolina, Virginia, and South Carolina from the Colonial Period to About 1820.* 4th edition. 2 vols. Baltimore: Clearfield Company, 2001.

> ————. *Free African Americans of Maryland and Delaware from the Colonial Period to 1810.* Baltimore: Clearfield Co., 2000.

While the latter volume technically falls outside the realm that is generally considered to be the American Southeast, a significant number of families featured in it overlap with those of colonies and states to the South.

PART TWO

EARLY FEDERAL RECORDS

CHAPTER 3

HISTORICAL &
GENEALOGICAL CHANGES

I t is often said that Native American genealogy is a study of "white men's records." To a large degree, the saying is true. Aside from the Cherokee, Indian language was exclusively oral and, so too, was tribal history.[36] While oral accounts are invaluable to understanding a people's sense of self and socialization, their reliability for genealogy seldom extends beyond the most recent generations. For research on the historic Indian tribes of the American Southeast, documentary evidence falls into two major groups: materials created by the United States and those created by other governments and entities.

Prior pages introduced resources and perspectives for researching Southeastern Indian families; the present section continues that discussion. The previous chapter examined nonfederal records created by the Spanish, French, and English colonies and by the *state* governments prior to the 1830s and 1840s, when most of the Southeastern Indians were removed to Indian Territory. Chapters 3 and 4 focus upon federal records. The spotlight remains on the states east of the Mississippi. However, because remnants of these tribes remained in the Southeastern states after the forced exodus, these final chapters include some events through 1931—the year in which the last "Final Roll" was approved for the major Southeastern tribes.

The scope of available federal records is too vast to cover in any one guide. This one focuses upon resources that can help researchers (*a*) make genealogical connections that may not be possible from conventional resources and (b) prove or disprove rumored tribal connections.

HISTORICAL BACKGROUND

The five Indian groups that dominated the Southeast, known to history as the Five Civilized Tribes, were not all of the same ethnic family. The Cherokee were the southernmost branch of the Iroquois. Choctaws, Chickasaws, Creeks, and Seminoles were dominant members of the Muskogean family. Beyond these, several other tribes were still viable in the Lower South as the United States government moved into and across that area—for example, the Catawba in South Carolina and the Koasati (Coushatta) in Alabama—although federal records of the late-eighteenth and nineteenth centuries largely ignore these smaller groups.[37]

In Arkansas and Louisiana, states normally considered part of the Southeastern United States, other tribes were active. However, the major groups there (the Caddo and Osage) were culturally akin to the tribes of the Southwest and the Plains. Smaller groups—remnants of the Attakapas, Chitimachas, Taensa, and Tunica, for example—had exceedingly limited relations with the United States until the twentieth century; thus, little is found on them in the earlier federal records. However, by the time the United States had acquired this area, via the Louisiana Purchase of 1803, small bands from the Five Civilized Tribes were already migrating into Arkansas and Louisiana, first to hunt and then to settle.[38]

Federal relations with America's native peoples were both paternalistic and antagonistic. Consequently, the surviving historical records were kept for a variety of purposes: to subdue and subjugate tribes; to effect and maintain treaties; to minimize conflict between Indians and whites (and blacks); to acquire territory; to identify and compensate individual Indians and white countrymen displaced by land transfers; to remove tribes; to educate and assimilate individuals; and, of course, to financially support whole groups after they were reduced to welfare status by Euro-American encroachment.

CHRONOLOGICAL FRAMEWORK

Premodern records of federal interaction with American Indians are divided broadly into three bureaucratic periods. A basic familiarity with these political time divisions is essential to the location of federal records.[39]

1774–1789: Pre-Federal Era

September 1774 saw the first assembly of the Continental Congress, a body that would govern until the individual colonies adopted the Articles of Confederation in 1781. From then until the creation of the United States in 1789, the union was governed by Confederation congresses, which created three separate Indian superintendencies to serve the Southern, Middle, and Northern tribes. The records of this era are maintained separately from the federal records below.

1789–1824: War Department Era

With the creation of the United States in 1789, Indian affairs were assigned to the Department of War, where authority would remain for the next thirty-five years. *Most records in the War Department were destroyed by fire on 8 November 1800.* Consequently, for genealogical purposes, most "Indian records" within this department date only from 1800–24. In 1806, an Office of Indian Trade was established within the War Department—a bureaucratic move that caused another regrouping of records.

1824–1947: Bureau of Indian Affairs (BIA) Era

In March 1824, the War Department established a separate Office (later Bureau) of Indian Affairs—generally known today as the BIA.[40] This office functioned until 1849, when it was moved to the Department of the Interior.

Hence, those "Indian records" genealogists seek at the National Archives are scattered across several collections, according to time frame: i.e., the records of the Continental Congress, the War Department, and the BIA.[41] Most extant records of the Continental Congress have been published in print or microform, with excellent indexes. For the War Department era, resources are more limited and far less easily explored. Under the BIA, vast resources have been created, and major ones now have finding aids and published transcripts or abstracts. Yet many researchers who use them to search for Southeastern Indian forebears are disappointed, because the BIA materials on these tribes predominantly relate to families that removed to Oklahoma.

This chapter selects material from all three of the above administrations, to create a focused catalog of federal holdings most productive for work on Southeastern Indians who did *not* migrate westward.

TOPICAL FRAMEWORK

Typically, genealogists approach federal Indian records from the tribal standpoint. General research or family tradition persuades them that they have a likely affiliation with a specific tribe, and so they seek tribal records to prove or disprove that connection. The catalog of records that forms chapter 4 and the selective bibliography both follow those tribal groups. However, the structure of the records and the issues that created them often transcend tribal bounds—particularly where Southeastern tribes are concerned in the following areas:

Agencies vs. Factories

Initially, federal interest in Native Americans was divided into two broad categories: matters relating to trade and those relating to all else. Thus, there developed a dual system of administration:

AGENCIES (AND SUPERINTENDENCIES)

Early U.S. Indian policy, in a sense, was an extension of English policy that considered each tribe a "nation," to be dealt with independently. In that context, the federal government placed "diplomatic posts" among each of the major tribes and appointed agents who were to keep peace on the frontier and otherwise represent the interests of the United States. Centralized superintendencies oversaw the agencies; their number and location varied across time. Genealogists seeking Indian forebears in the Southeast will have minimal involvement with superintendency records but should be aware of their existence.

The agency system developed gradually after 1792. By the time of the removal, agencies existed among all the Five Civilized Tribes. Smaller tribes in the Southeast were not assigned separate agencies; problems involving them were generally handled by whatever other agency existed in their area.[42] Figure 5 identifies these Southeastern agencies, their geographic bases, and their years of operation.

Figure 5

Federal Indian Agencies in the Southeastern United States

YEARS	NAME	HEADQUARTERS
1792	Cherokee Agency East	East Central Tennessee
1813–1817	Cherokee Agency West [Subagency of Cherokee East]	Arkansas & White Rivers, Arkansas
1800–1839	Chickasaw Agency	Northeast Mississippi
1792–1832	Choctaw Agency East	Various sites, Alabama & Mississippi
1792–1836	Creek Agency East	Various sites, Georgia & Alabama

Extracted from Edward E. Hill, *Records of the Bureau of Indian Affairs*, Preliminary Inventory no. 163, 2 vols. (Washington: National Archives and Records Service, 1965), 2: 304–5, 308–9, 311, 347–50, 352–53, 358.

FACTORIES (AND TRADERS)

From 1795 until the early 1820s, the U.S. operated a system of Indian trading posts called *factories*. Tribal allegiance during the previous century, when three European governments vied for control of the Southeastern tribes, had depended upon the value and variety of trade goods that the competing governments could supply. As the U.S. government replaced the foreign ones and tried to stabilize its relations with Native American nations, the factory system was a critical diplomatic tool.

The agents who were placed in charge—called *factors* to distinguish them from the "regular" agents—were also responsible for distributing annual payments (*annuities*) to tribes who had officially surrendered land to the United States. Supporting the factors was a network of supply agents operating out of the major commercial centers, primarily New Orleans, St. Louis, and Savannah for the Southeast trade. Although the system officially ended in 1822, some factory records extend past that point, as figure 6 shows.

In addition to the factors, private traders also continued to operate within the tribes, as they had under the colonial governments. From 1786 forward, they were licensed by the various superintendents and agents, under the dominion of the Secretary of War.[43]

Removal and Reserves

The Louisiana Purchase of 1803 was politically popular for several reasons. Among others, it added to the United States vast lands to which Indian tribes east of the Mississippi River could be removed. Official federal pressure upon the tribes to abandon their eastern lands dates from the Cherokee Treaty of 1817, which provided for voluntary relocation. By congressional act of 28 May 1830, the removal of all Indian tribes to the West became the government's official policy. That objective was largely realized by the mid-1840s, but government-sponsored removal continued as late as 1871.[44]

Figure 6

Factories (U.S. Government Trading Posts)

YEARS	NAME	LOCATION
1805–1810	Arkansas	Arkansas River
1795–1807	Cherokee	Tellico, in East Central Tennessee
1807–1810	" "	Hiwassee, Tennessee River, Tennessee
1802–1818	Chickasaw Bluffs	Near Memphis, Tennessee
1802–1815	Choctaw	Ft. St. Stephens, above Mobile, Alabama
1815–1825	" "	Ft. Confederation, Tombigbee River, Alabama
1795–1797	Creek	Colerain, St. Mary's River, Georgia
1797–1806	" "	Ft. Wilkinson, Georgia
1806–1809	" "	Ocmulgee Old Fields, Georgia
1809–1816	" "	Ft. Hawkins, Georgia
1816–1820	" "	Ft. Mitchell, Alabama
1805–1818	Natchitoches	Natchitoches, Red River, Louisiana
1818–1823	Sulphur Fork	Sulphur Fork, Red River, Arkansas
1818–1824	Spadre Bluffs	Illinois Bayou, Arkansas

Extracted from Hill, *Records of the Bureau of Indian Affairs*, 1: 18–19, 23–31.

However, total removal never occurred. Various treaties allowed individual Indians (and whites and blacks with Indian spouses and children) to remain behind on *reserves* assigned to individual households. Some of those who elected to stay behind were driven out by unscrupulous whites and either moved on to Indian Territory or banded together in remote, unsettled areas from North Carolina to Florida to Louisiana. Some others who went west eventually returned to the neighborhoods of their birth. Consequently, federal interaction with Indian tribes and bands east of the Mississippi has continued even to the present day.[45]

Post-removal Records

For generations after the mass exodus took place, the relocated families were embroiled in other events and circumstances that created files of immense genealogical value—even for descendants of individuals who did not move. Two such situations were the creation of "final rolls" for each of the Five Civilized Tribes and the settlement of various types of claims that individuals or tribes held against the United States.

FINAL ROLLS

Removing the Indian nations to the west of the Mississippi did not halt the frontier's encroachment upon them. By the late-nineteenth century, tens of thousands of interlopers and several railroads occupied tribal lands in Oklahoma, with or without permission. The fact that tribal lands were held in common prevented intruders from obtaining legal titles to the tracts they coveted. Pressure mounted upon Congress to force the Native American nations into a system of private land ownership that would enable enterprising whites to buy or otherwise acquire deeds to individual tracts.

From 1887 through the turn of the century, a series of congressional acts implemented this objective. The General Allotment Act of 1887 made it a federal policy to see that each individual Indian had his or her own allotment of land. In 1893, Congress established the Commission to the Five Civilized Tribes—familiarly known as the Dawes Commission—with a mandate to renegotiate land policies with the Oklahoma nations. An added mandate in 1896 called for the commission to compile rolls identifying all individuals who could prove their rightful membership in each of the tribes and would thus be qualified to share in the eventual division of the lands.[46]

Over the next two decades, as the Five Civilized Tribes were forced to capitulate, these mandates created a mass of genealogical records that are surely unparalleled in American history—records that treat not only the Oklahoma tribes but also the Eastern Cherokee (based in North Carolina), the Mississippi Choctaw, and thousands of individuals who acknowledged or claimed a family tradition of descent from one of these tribes, even though their forebears had severed tribal ties.

The value of the genealogical and historical information is greatly enhanced by the commission's decision to enroll individuals in eight separate categories:[47]

- Citizens by Blood
- Citizens by Marriage
- New Born Citizens by Blood
- Minor Citizens by Blood
- Freedmen (African Americans whom the Indians had held in slavery but later freed and admitted to tribal membership)
- New Born Freedmen
- Minor Freedmen
- Delaware Indians Adopted by the Cherokee

Three types of cards were generally kept within each enrollment category:

"STRAIGHT" CARDS:	persons whose applications had been approved
"D" CARDS:	persons whose eligibility was considered doubtful at time of enrollment and who were, thus, subject to more investigation
"R" CARDS:	persons whose applications had been rejected

While variations exist, cards generally offer the following:

- Name, roll number
- Age, sex, degree of Indian blood
- Relationship to head of the family group

- Names of parents
- References to enrollment on earlier rolls
- Miscellaneous notes regarding (a) births, deaths, and marriages; and (b) actions and decisions by the commission and the Interior Department

CLAIM SETTLEMENTS

Throughout the course of history, claims and the need to settle them have been an incessant problem of Indian-white relations. The various guides to the National Archives (NARA) records cited in this book describe seemingly endless types of cases; but three of these deserve special note for the wealth of now-easily accessible materials that the claims process generated.

Choctaw Net Proceeds Case (1875–89, 1897–98)

By terms of the Treaty of Dancing Rabbit Creek, which the United States executed with the Choctaw Nation in 1830, the U.S. was to sell the lands relinquished by the Choctaw and a portion of the net proceeds was to be distributed among tribal members. By 1875, that distribution still had not been made. Additionally, many individuals and families in the Nation had long-outstanding claims against the federal government for houses and other improvements on the eastern land they had to abandon, for expenses occurred in emigrating, and for other losses. In 1875 the Choctaw launched a series of ultimately successful suits against the United States in the federal courts, which proceeded through appeals to the U.S. Court of Claims and the U.S. Supreme Court. While the Oklahoma Choctaw were the instigators of the suit, the resulting records are rich in details on their Mississippi and Alabama ancestors and collateral kin.[48]

Guion Miller Enrollment of Eastern Cherokee (1906–10)

Under the treaties of 1835, 1836, and 1845, the Cherokee who chose to remain in the East as a splinter tribe were also to receive certain monetary awards for the relinquishment of their lands. In the wake of a 1902–6 suit by the Cherokee against the U.S., the Court of Claims appointed Guion Miller as Special Commissioner to identify all individuals who should share in the awards. Applications for enrollment were accepted throughout 1907 and 1908. The files that support Miller's final report of 1909 represent a rich gold mine of genealogical data—both proved and claimed but unproved.[49]

Special Files

One of the more valuable—and more neglected—collections held by the Bureau of Indian Affairs is a miscellaneous assortment of materials called "Special Files." Officially dated 1807–1904, the accounts, affidavits, correspondence, reports, and other records in this collection relate primarily to such claims as those of

- traders for goods furnished to Indians or to the government
- transportation contractors for shipping services
- attorneys for legal fees
- individuals for services to Indians or to the government
- Indians and whites for losses from depredations committed by the other
- Indians for losses resulting from their removal from the East
- persons claiming the right to share in tribal benefits

Materials in the files have been withdrawn from other collections. Most are from general incoming correspondence of the Indian Office; but some are records of special commissions, transmitted to the office when their work was completed. In general, each file relates to a single subject. The inclusive dates that NARA assigns to this collection (1807–1904) mainly represent "the date of receipt in the office or by a commission." The documents therein may date considerably further back in time.[50]

The abundance of records created by the agencies, factories, claims, enrollments, removals, and reserves is cataloged in chapter 4.

RESEARCH PROCEDURES

Research in federal records can be intimidating and overwhelming—or it can be a logical, practical, and rewarding process. Success depends upon basically four things:

1. Understanding the economic, political, and social conditions that caused particular records to be created

2. Knowing what records exist

3. Knowing how and where to find these records

4. Knowing how to use them

The first goal is accomplished by well-rounded study in sound historical works. The earlier chapters discuss a number of the conditions and suggests many excellent monographs. More are added in the reference notes to the present section and the bibliography.[51] The remaining goals are accomplished by studying the numerous finding aids that catalog and more or less describe millions of records held by the National Archives in Washington, D.C., and in two of its regional facilities: NARA's Southeast Region (Atlanta, Georgia); and NARA's Southwest Region (Fort Worth, Texas). Most of these guides are currently in print and available for purchase at a modest cost.[52] Some may be downloaded from the National Archives web site <http://www.nara.gov>.

FINDING AIDS

All serious researchers in the field of Native American genealogy and history will want to acquire the following reference works for their personal libraries:

HARDBACK GUIDES (NARRATIVE DISCUSSIONS)

Hill, Edward E. *Guide to Records in the National Archives of the United States Relating to American Indians.* Washington: National Archives and Records Service (NARS), 1981. 467 pp. Covers virtually all territory within the bounds of the continental United States and most tribes active from the formation of the U.S. government.

Eales, Anne Bruner, and Robert M. Kvasnicka. *Guide to Genealogical Research in the National Archives*. 3d ed. Washington: National Archives Trust Fund Board, 2000. Chapter 11 of this publication provides a useful summation of records most often needed by family historians seeking Indian ancestry.

DOCUMENT CATALOGS

Hill, Edward E. *Records of the Bureau of Indian Affairs*. Preliminary Inventory no. 163. 2 vols. Washington: NARS, 1965. 459 pp. Offers brief background on the Bureau and various agencies within it, along with paragraph-length descriptions of 1,401 record collections. Details include a general description of contents, relevant dates, and collection size.

MAP CATALOGS

Kelsay, Laura E. *Cartographic Records of the Bureau of Indian Affairs*. Special List 13. Washington: NARS, 1977. 187 pp. Offers brief descriptions of each of 977 items or groups of items—land plats, maps, blueprints, surveys, quadrangle sheets, etc.—covering virtually all tribes in the continental U.S.

MICROFILM CATALOGS

American Indians: A Select Catalog of National Archives Microfilm Publications. Washington: National Archives Trust Fund Board, 1998. 139 pp. Regularly updated. Presently itemizes 212 collections from the War Department and the BIA, as well as such civilian agencies as the Census Bureau; Congressional Court of Claims; Interior, State, and Treasury Departments; Geological Survey; and Fish and Wildlife Service.

A companion work, commercially produced, offers a valuable guide to relevant holdings of the regional archives in Atlanta and Fort Worth:

Szucs, Loretto Dennis, and Sandra Hargreaves Luebking. *The Archives: A Guide to the National Archives Field Branches*. Salt Lake City: Ancestry, 1988.

Figure 7

A Step-by-Step Procedure for
Locating Indian Records in the National Archives

1. Conduct "normal" research until evidence suggests a likely Indian connection at a specific time, with a specific tribe, and in a specific place.

2. Study corresponding sections of the two guides by Hill.

3. Make master list of all records or collections found in the guides that seem to be relevant.

4. Check the microfilm catalog for each item.

   A. If the materials are on film, note whether the description includes DP. This indicates that a *descriptive pamphlet* has been created to more fully describe the collection.

   Typically, the pamphlet will give background information on the records, list each roll in the publication, and provide a one-line description of the contents of that roll.

   In some cases, the DP provides nothing more than what appears in the American Indian microfilm catalog. In other cases, it provides far more. The DP itself should always be examined.

   1) Order the free DP from NARA's sales office, if it is in print. If not in print, then order that microfilm publication's first roll, on which the DP is found.

   2) Identify and order appropriate film. Expect to work with unindexed manuscripts.

   B. If the materials are not microfilmed, go to step 5.

5. Reexamine Hill's preliminary inventory of original documents to determine the size of the relevant collection and the way in which it is organized.

   A. If the collection is indexed or alphabetized, a concise inquiry to the National Archives *might* generate a search by the staff.

   This inquiry should identify (a) the specific record group (by number and name); (b) the specific "entry" (number and name) from the preliminary inventory; and (c) the name of the individual for which the index should be checked.

   B. If the collection is large and unindexed, a personal search on-site is necessary.

CHAPTER 4

FEDERAL RECORDS:
MANUSCRIPTS, BOOKS & FILMS

A side from the chronological and topical matters previously discussed, records pertinent to the Five Civilized Tribes were basically created at two levels: the central administration in Washington and the field agencies. The following catalog of resources presents, first, a series of central-administration records of key value; then second, the field-agency records, by tribe.

CENTRAL-ADMINISTRATION RECORDS:
NOT DIVIDED BY TRIBE

PRE-FEDERAL ERA

M247 *Papers of the Continental Congress, 1774–1789.* 204 rolls. DP. Particularly see

Roll 65: Florida, Letters and Reports from Indian Agents and Commissioners

Roll 85: Virginia, State Papers

Roll 86: North and South Carolina, State Papers

Roll 87: Georgia, State Papers

M332   *Miscellaneous Papers of the Continental Congress, 1774–1789.* 9 rolls. DP.

For an index, see:

Butler, John P., comp. *Index: The Papers of the Continental Congress, 1774–1789.* 5 vols. Washington: NARS, 1978.[53]

FEDERAL ERA

Bureau (Office) of Indian Affairs

M18   *Registers of Letters Received, 1824–1880.* 126 rolls.

These registers "index" (somewhat) the microfilm series M234, *Letters Received, Office of Indian Affairs, 1824–1881*, which is cited below and under the specific tribes. Registers were created in chronological order. Entries in each are alphabetical by name of writer and provide the file number needed to locate the letter in M234.

Not all the letters registered in M18 are actually filed with the Office of Indian Affairs. According to Hill, "Many of them were referred to the Secretary of War, the Secretary of the Interior, the Second Auditor, or some other official outside of the Bureau. . . . Letters that went back and forth several times between the Bureau and the . . . Secretary of the Interior are most probably now among the records of the Bureau. They may be filed either in their original place or as an enclosure to a letter from the Secretary."[54]

M234   *Letters Received, Office of Indian Affairs, 1824–1881.* 962 rolls. For an index, see *Registers of Letters Received, 1824–1880*, M18 above.

Rolls 772–77: Schools, 1824–36

M574   *Special Files, 1807–1904.* 85 rolls.

The Descriptive Pamphlet to M574 itemizes each file. The labels to some files explicitly carry the name of a tribe.

Figure 8

Selective Table

National Archives Record Groups Treating American Indians

RECORD GROUP (RG) NUMBER	NAME
22	Records of the Fish and Wildlife Service
29	" " Bureau of the Census
48	Department of the Interior
49	General Land Office
56	Department of the Treasury
57	Geological Survey
59	Department of State
75	Bureau of Indian Affairs
94	Adjutant General's Office
107	Office of the Secretary of State
108	Headquarters of the Army
109	War Department Collection of Confederate Records
153	Office of the Judge Advocate General
167	Supreme Court of the United States
360	Continental Congress and Constitutional Convention

Others labels carry the names of individuals, who may be white, Indian, or black.

Dawes Commission

Some very useful resources treating this key subject are not subdivided by tribe. Among the most important which researchers will not want to overlook are the following:[55]

[Manuscripts.] Docket Books for the Five Civilized Tribes, 1897–1910. 41 vols. 3 linear ft. Entry 306, RG 75. Arranged in part by subject and in part chronologically.

[Manuscripts.] Records Relating to Applications for Enrollment from the Five Civilized Tribes, 1910–15. 1 ft. Entry 607, RG 75.

M1314 *Index to Letters Received by the Commission to the Five Civilized Tribes, 1897–1913.* 23 rolls. The original records, once identified through this index, can be obtained from the NARA's Southwest.

Secretary of the Interior, Indian Division

M606 *Letters Sent, 1849–1903.* 127 rolls. DP. Arrangement is generally chronological; indexes are on rolls 121–27.

M825 *Selected Classes of Letters Received by the Indian Division of the Office of the Secretary of the Interior, 1849–1880.* 32 rolls. DP.

War Department

M15 *Letters Sent by the Secretary of War Relating to Indian Affairs, 1800–1824.* 6 rolls. Covers agents, factors, missionaries, passports, traders, etc. Generally indexed.

M16 *Letters Sent, Superintendent of Indian Trade, 1807–1823.* 6 rolls. Contains correspondence from agents, bankers, factors, manufacturers, and merchants, regarding annuity payments; employment applications and appointments; supplies and trade goods; etc. Indexed by name of addressee.

M221 *Letters Received by the Secretary of War, Main Series, 1801–1870.* 317 rolls. DP. Arranged by date blocks, thereunder by file number given in the register. Only a small fraction of the Indian material in this series is reproduced as M15 and M271.

M222   *Letters Received by the Secretary of War, Unregistered Series, 1789–1861.* 34 rolls. DP. Arranged by year, thereunder alphabetically—usually by initial letter of surname or office of writer, sometimes by initial letter of subject.

M271   *Letters Received by the Secretary of War Relating to Indian Affairs, 1800–1823.* 4 rolls. Predominantly treats Southeastern Indians and the Northern Seneca. Arranged chronologically, then alphabetically by name of writer.

T58   *Letters Received, Superintendent of Indian Trade, 1800–1824.* 1 roll. Offers manuscript, record-book copies of letters sent from the Office of Indian Trade and those of the agent appointed by the War Department to liquidate the factories. The subject matter parallels that of *Letters Sent.* Mostly chronological.

[Manuscripts.] Index to Ledger, 1807–16, General Accounting Records, Superintendent of Indian Trade. 1 vol., ¼ in. Entry 10, RG 75. This is a beginning point to four dozen or so volumes, as well as to some loose records—with the various factories intermingled—that exist as Entries 5–26 in RG 75. For an introduction, see the discussion in Hills's preliminary inventory of the BIA records.[56]

MISCELLANEOUS PUBLICATIONS

American State Papers: Documents Legislative and Executive of the Congress of the United States. 38 vols. Washington: Gales and Seaton, 1832–61. Particularly see the following series:

- Indian Affairs Series, vols. 1–2 [with material dating 1789–1827]
- Military Affairs Series, vol. 6, pp. 450–781
- Public Lands Series, vols. 1–8 [with material dating back to the 1700s]

RECORDS: BY TRIBE

CHEROKEE

Agency Records:

M208   *Records of the Cherokee Indian Agency in Tennessee, 1801–1835.* 14 rolls. DP. Includes all Eastern Cherokee settlements in this period, regardless of locale.

M1059 *Selected Letters Received by the Office of Indian Affairs Relating to the Cherokees of North Carolina, 1851–1905.* 7 rolls. DP.

[Manuscripts.] Records of the Cherokee Agency East. Entries 1041–56, RG 75. 23 vols. and ca. 2 ft. of unbound papers. Includes accounts, affidavits, claims for losses and military service, correspondence, an emigration list, journals, passports, receipts, rolls, and supply contracts. Some of this is reproduced on M208.[57]

Censuses and Enrollments:

M595   *Indian Census Rolls, 1885–1940.* 692 rolls. DP. See

Rolls 22–25: Cherokee (North Carolina), 1898–99, 1904, 1906, 1909–12, 1914–32

M685   *Records Relating to Enrollment of the Eastern Cherokee by Guion Miller, 1908–1910.* 12 rolls. DP. See especially

Roll 1: Index to subsequent rolls

Roll 12: Copies of the Drennen, Chapman, and Old Settler rolls (1851–52) and the Hester Roll (1884), with indexes

M1104 *Eastern Cherokee Applications of the U.S. Court of Claims, 1906–1909.* 348 rolls. DP. An index appears on roll 1.[58]

M1186 *Enrollment Cards of the Five Civilized Tribes, 1898–1914.* 93 rolls. DP. See especially

Roll 1: Index to the Final Rolls

Rolls 2–38: Cherokee enrollment cards

M1301 *Applications for Enrollment of the Commission to the Five Civilized Tribes, 1898–1914.* 468 rolls. These applications contain extensive materials not abstracted on the enrollment cards. The order within each tribal group is numerical, corresponding to the enrollment numbers the cards supply. See

Rolls 174–399: Cherokee applications and memos (Act of 1900)

T496 *Census Roll, 1835, of Cherokee Indians East of the Mississippi, with Index.* 1 roll. (The so-called Henderson Roll)

T529 *Final Rolls of Citizens and Freedmen of the Five Civilized Tribes in Indian Territory.* 3 rolls. Includes names of both approved and disapproved individuals. Arranged first by tribe, then by category, then alphabetically.[59] See

Roll 2: Cherokee rolls

[Manuscripts.] The Guion Miller Enrollment Records, 1902–1911. 34 vols. and ca. 12 ft. of unbound papers. Includes applications, indexes, reports, transcripts of testimony, copies of past census rolls (including an undated supplement to the 1851 Siler Roll and a 1910 supplement to the 1906 roll of Eastern Cherokee).[60]

[Manuscripts.] Census Rolls, 1835–69. 5 in. Entry 676, RG 75. Eastern Cherokee.[61]

[Manuscripts.] Eastern Cherokee Census Rolls, 1835–84. 5 in. Entry 219, RG 75. Includes Henderson (1835, pre-removal), Mullay (1848), Siler (1851), Chapman (1852), Powell (1867, unindexed), Swetland (1869, partially unindexed), and Hester (1884).[62]

[Manuscripts.] Cherokee Indian Agency, Cherokee, North Carolina, 1886–1952. Includes agency censuses (1898–1902), correspondence, and school files and reports (1889–52). Now housed at NARA's Southeast Region.[63]

[Manuscripts.] Records Relating to Enrollment of Eastern Cherokee, 1907–1931. 44 vols. and ca. 19 ft. of unbound papers. Entries 590–603, RG 75. Includes affidavits, applications, correspondence, indexes, reports, and 1907–9 rolls of the Eastern Band.[64]

Central Office (D.C.) Records:

M234 *Letters Received, Office of Indian Affairs, 1824–1881.* 962 rolls. DP. For an index, see M18, previously cited under general works on all tribes (p. 258). For actual letters, see

Rolls 71–76: Cherokee Agency, East, 1824–36

Rolls 113–18: Cherokee emigration and reserves, 1828–50

M1059 *Selected Letters Received by the Office of Indian Affairs Relating to the Cherokees of North Carolina, 1851–1905.* 7 rolls. DP.

M1070 *Reports of Inspection of the Field Jurisdictions of the Office of Indian Affairs, 1873–1900.* 60 rolls. DP. See

Roll 11: Eastern Cherokee Agency

Factory Records:

[Manuscripts.] Miscellaneous Accounts, 1796–1810. 5 in. Entry 34, RG 75.[65]

Miscellaneous Records:

[Manuscripts.] Records Concerning Traders' Claims, ca. 1819–64. 66 vols. and unbound papers. Entry 893, RG 75. Includes Eastern Cherokee, among others.[66]

Removal Records:

[Manuscripts.] Cherokee Removal Records, 1817–84. 99 vols. and unbound papers. Entries 217–51, RG 75. Includes account books, applications, and registers of Indians who wished to remain in the East as citizens, Eastern Cherokee census rolls (1835–84), claim files and registers, emigration rolls, land certificates and sales, property valuations, etc.[67]

Reserves Records:

[Manuscripts.] Docket Book, Claims Papers, Decisions, 1837–39. 2 vols. and ca. 5 in. of unbound papers. Entries 228–30, RG 75.[68]

[Manuscripts.] Reports Concerning Private Claims Affecting Lands of Eastern Cherokees, 1916. ¼ in. Entry 567, RG 75. Includes maps of Cherokee landholdings in several North Carolina counties.[69]

[Manuscripts.] Schedules Concerning Per Capita Payments to Removed Cherokee, 1871–73. 1 in. Entry 630, RG 75. Includes lists of Eastern Indians paid to move to Indian Territory in 1871.[70]

CHICKASAW

Agency Records:

[Manuscripts.] Records of the Chickasaw Agency East, 1812–16. Entry 1058, RG 75. ¼ in. Includes letters, receipts, vouchers.[71]

Note: See also Cherokee Agency records for other Chickasaw materials of the early 1800s.

Censuses and Enrollments:

M1186 Enrollment Cards of the Five Civilized Tribes, 1898–1914. 93 rolls. DP. See especially

Roll 1: Index to the Final Rolls

Rolls 67–76: Chickasaw enrollments [sundry categories]

M1301 *Applications for Enrollment of the Commission to the Five Civilized Tribes, 1898–1914.* 468 rolls. Contains much personal information not abstracted on enrollment cards. Arranged by tribe; then numerical, by enrollment number. See

Rolls 172–73: Choctaw-Chickasaw memos (Act 1902)

Rolls 434–68: Chickasaw applications (various)

T529 *Final Rolls of Citizens and Freedmen of the Five Civilized Tribes in Indian Territory.* 3 rolls. Includes names of both approved and disapproved individuals. Arranged first by tribe, then by category, then alphabetically. See

Roll 1: Chickasaw and Choctaw rolls

[Manuscripts.] Census and Muster Rolls, 1837–39. Entry 253, RG 75. 1 in.[72]

Central Office (D.C.) Records:

M234 *Letters Received, Office of Indian Affairs, 1824–1881.* 962 rolls. DP. For index, see M18, cited under general works treating all tribes (p. 258). For actual letters, see

Rolls 135–37: Chickasaw Agency [East], 1824–39

Rolls 143–44: Chickasaw Agency emigration, 1837–50

Rolls 145–48: Chickasaw Agency reserves, 1836–50

Factory Records:

CHICKASAW BLUFFS FACTORY

[Manuscripts.] Daybooks, 1806–7, 1 in.; Miscellaneous Accounts, 1807–18, 4 in. Entries 38–39, RG 75.[73]

[Manuscripts.] Accounts of the U.S. "Factory" at Chickasaw Bluffs, Quarter Ending March 31, 1811. Less than ¼ in. Entry 264, RG 59.[74]

SPADRE BLUFFS FACTORY

(Replaced Chickasaw Bluffs in 1818)
[Manuscripts.] Miscellaneous Accounts, 1805–23, 10 in. Entry 73, RG 75.[75]

Removal Records:

[Manuscripts.] Chickasaw Removal Records, 1832–61. 5 vols. Entries 252–57, RG 75. Includes correspondence, land locations and sales, ledgers, etc.[76]

Reserves Records:

[CD]   *Automated Records Project; Pre-1908 Patents—Homesteads, Cash Entry, Choctaw Indian Scrip, and Chickasaw Cession Lands: Mississippi.* CD-ROM. Springfield, Virginia: Bureau of Land Management, Eastern States, 1996.

[Manuscripts.] Abstracts of Locations of Land, Reports of Land Sales and Deeds, Statements Concerning Proceeds, 1836–49. 3 vols. and 1 in. of unbound papers. Entries 254–55, 257, RG 75.[77]

CHOCTAW

Agency Records:

[Manuscripts.] Records of the Choctaw Agency East, 1817–21. Entry 1059, RG 75. Unbound papers of less than ¼ in. Includes letters, list of employees, vouchers.[78]

Censuses and Enrollments:

M595   *Indian Census Rolls, 1885–1940.* 692 rolls. DP. See especially Rolls 41–42: Choctaw (Mississippi), 1926–39

M1186 *Enrollment Cards of the Five Civilized Tribes, 1898–1914.* 93 rolls. DP. See

Roll 1: Index to the Final Rolls

Rolls 39–56: Choctaw enrollments [various categories]

Rolls 56–66: Mississippi Choctaw enrollments [various]

M1301 *Applications for Enrollment of the Commission to the Five Civilized Tribes, 1898–1914.* 468 rolls. These applications contain extensive materials not abstracted on the enrollment cards. The order within each tribal group is numerical, corresponding to the enrollment numbers that the cards supply. See

Rolls 1–82: Choctaw applications [various categories]

Rolls 82–171: Mississippi Choctaw applications

Rolls 172–73: Choctaw-Chickasaw memos (Act 1902; index on roll 172)

T529 *Final Rolls of Citizens and Freedmen of the Five Civilized Tribes in Indian Territory.* 3 rolls. Includes names of both approved and disapproved individuals. Arranged first by tribe, then by category, then alphabetically. See

Roll 1: Choctaw and Chickasaw rolls (including Mississippi Choctaw)

[Manuscripts.] Census Rolls, 1831, 1856. 1 vol. and ¼ in. of unbound papers. Entries 258, 260, RG 75. Better known, respectively, as Armstrong and Cooper Rolls of Eastern Choctaw.[79]

[Manuscripts.] Records Relating to Applications for Identification as Mississippi Choctaw, 1901–7. 17 ft. of unbound papers. Entry 606, RG 75. Includes affidavits, applications, correspondence, petitions, etc.[80]

[Manuscripts.] Final Rolls of the Mississippi Choctaw. 4 ft., 20 vols. Entry 715, RG 48. Includes an 1898 roll of unproved Mississippi Choctaw claims.[81]

Central Office (D.C.) Records:

M234   *Letters Received, Office of Indian Affairs, 1824–1881.* 962 rolls. DP. For index, see M18, cited on p. 258. For actual letters, see

Rolls 168–70: Choctaw Agency [East], 1824–38

Rolls 185–87: Choctaw Agency emigration, 1826–59

Rolls 188–96: Choctaw Agency reserves, 1836–60

Factory Records:

T500   *Records of Choctaw Trading House, 1803–1824.* 6 rolls.[82]

Removal Records:

[Manuscripts.] Emigration lists, 1831–57. 5 vols. and unbound papers. Entry 261, RG 75.[83]

Reserves Records:

[CD]   United States, General Land Office. *Automated Records Project; Pre-1908 Patents—Homesteads, Cash Entry, Creek Indian Treaty, and Choctaw Indian Scrip: Alabama.* CD-ROM. Springfield, Virginia: Bureau of Land Management, Eastern States, 1996.

[CD]   *Automated Records Project; Pre-1908 Patents—Homesteads, Cash Entry, Choctaw Indian Scrip, and Chickasaw Cession Lands: Mississippi.* CD-ROM. Springfield, Virginia: Bureau of Land Management, Eastern States, 1996.

[Manuscripts.] Choctaw Scrip, 1830–54. 6 ft. Entry 23, RG 49. Covers certificates for acreage; also lists of located lands,

entries in conflict, and assignments and patents—all
stemming from reserves requested by individual Choctaw
under the Treaty of Dancing Rabbit Creek, 27 September
1830.[84]

[Manuscripts.] Papers Relating to Lands Located under Choctaw
Treaty of Sept. 27, 1830. 3 packages. Entry 39 (Nashville/
Huntsville land offices, ca.1809–61), RG 49. Includes
deeds from Choctaw Indians; deeds for land reserved
under Choctaw treaty; correspondence, location of reservations; records of patents; abstracts of conveyances;
and court records.[85]

[Manuscripts.] Choctaw Treaty of Sept. 27, 1830—Compilations:
115–38; Washington Meridian, Mississippi, 1807–61.
[Size not stated.] Entry 54, RG 49. Includes conveyances
by Choctaw Indians of land reserved for them under 1830
treaty, affidavits, applications for approval of assignments,
correspondence, etc.[86]

[Manuscripts.] Choctaw Reserves and Related Claims, 1832–49.
39 vols. and ca. 3 ft. of unbound papers. Entries 259, 262–
84, RG 75. Includes affidavits, applications, individual
family lists (children named), land locations, orphans'
land records, scrip, stubs; also many other records of the
Murray and Claiborne Commissions established to take
testimony regarding Choctaw Reserve Claims in the
1830s and 1840s.[87]

[Manuscripts.] Choctaw Net Proceeds Case, 1875–79, 1889. 23
vols. and ca. 3 ft. 9 in. of unbound papers. Entries 530–
43, RG 75. Includes affidavits, applications, individual
family lists (including children), land locations, orphans'
land records, scrip, stubs, etc., dating back to 1830s and
1840s.[88]

School Records:

[Manuscripts.] Letter from the Secretary of War: A Communication from the Commissioner of Indian Affairs, in respect to the manner in which certain stipulations in the Choctaw treaty of Dancing Rabbit Creek have been fulfilled, 1 March 1841. House Document 109, 26th Congress, 2d Sess. 179 pp.[89]

CREEKS

Agency Records:

[Manuscripts.] Correspondence and Other Records, 1794–1818. 1 in. Entry 1065, RG 75. Includes letters received, copies of letters sent, licenses to trade, vouchers, and other records. Generally arranged chronologically.[90]

Censuses and Enrollments:

M1186 *Enrollment Cards of the Five Civilized Tribes, 1898–1914.* 93 rolls. DP. See especially

Roll 1: Index to the Final Rolls

Rolls 77–91: Creek enrollments (various categories)

M1301 *Applications for Enrollment of the Commission to the Five Civilized Tribes, 1898–1914.* 468 rolls. These applications contain extensive materials not abstracted onto the enrollment cards. The order within each tribal group is numerical, corresponding to the enrollment numbers that the cards supply. See

Rolls 402–34: Creek applications (various categories)

T275 *Census of Creek Indians (Parsons and Abbott), 1832.* 1 roll.

T529 *Final Rolls of Citizens and Freedmen of the Five Civilized Tribes in Indian Territory.* 3 rolls. Includes names of both approved and disapproved individuals. Arranged first by tribe, then by category, then alphabetically. See

Roll 3: Creek and Seminole rolls

Central Office (D.C.) Records:

M234 *Letters Received, Office of Indian Affairs, 1824–1881.* 962 rolls. DP. For an index, see M18, previously cited under general works treating all tribes (p. 258). For actual letters, see

Rolls 219–25: Creek Agency [East], 1824–36

Rolls 237–40: Creek Agency Emigration, 1826–49

Rolls 241–48: Creek Agency Reserves, 1832–50

Factory Records:

M4 *Records of the Creek Trading House, 1795–1816.* 1 roll.

M1334 *Records of the Creek Factory of the Office of Indian Trade of the Bureau of Indian Affairs, 1795–1821.* 13 rolls.

[Manuscripts.] Creek Factory Records, 1795–1820. 28 vols. and ca. 3 ft. of unbound papers. Entries 42–53, RG 75.[91]

Miscellaneous Records:

American State Papers: Documents Legislative and Executive of the Congress of the United States. 38 vols. Washington: Gales and Seaton, 1832–61. Particularly see Military Affairs Series, vol. 6: 450–781, for Creek conflict with specific white families and individuals.

Removal Records:

[Manuscripts.] Creek Removal Records, 1833–38. 9 vols. Entries 285, 299, RG 75. Includes censuses (Parsons and Abbott, 1833), emigration lists, and subsistence and relief rolls.[92]

Reserves Records:

[CD]   United States, General Land Office. *Automated Records Project;
        Pre-1908 Patents—Homesteads, Cash Entry, Creek Indian
        Treaty, and Choctaw Indian Scrip: Alabama.* CD-ROM.
        Springfield, Virginia: Bureau of Land Management, Eastern
        States, 1996.

[Manuscripts.] Creek Reserve Records, 1827–59. 24 vols. and 1 ft. 9
        in. of unbound papers. Entries 286–98, 300, RG 75. Includes
        index to reservees, land locations and sales, reports on deceased
        and defrauded reservees, etc.[93]

[Manuscripts.] Records Relating to the Sally Ladiga Case, 1836–57.
        ½ in. of unbound papers. Entry 566, RG 75. Letters and
        transcripts of legal proceedings.[94]

[Manuscripts.] Papers relating to Creek Indian Lands, 1832–46;
        Nashville/Huntsville land offices, ca.1809–61. 3 packages.
        Entry 39, RG 49. Includes certificates, contracts, correspon-
        dence, sales.[95]

SEMINOLES

Censuses and Enrollments:

M595   *Indian Census Rolls, 1885–1940.* 692 rolls. DP. See especially
        Roll 486–87: Seminole (Florida), 1913–40

M1186   *Enrollment Cards of the Five Civilized Tribes, 1898–1914.* 93
        rolls. DP. See especially
        Roll 1: Index to the Final Rolls
        Rolls 92–93: Seminole enrollments (various categories)

M1301   *Applications for Enrollment of the Commission to the Five Civilized
        Tribes, 1898–1914.* 468 rolls. These applications contain ex-
        tensive materials not abstracted on the enrollment cards. The
        order within each tribal group is numerical, corresponding to
        the enrollment numbers that the cards supply. See

Rolls 400–402: Seminole applications [various categories]

T529   *Final Rolls of Citizens and Freedmen of the Five Civilized Tribes in Indian Territory.* 3 rolls. Includes names of both approved and disapproved individuals. Arranged first by tribe, then by category, then alphabetically. See

Roll 3: Seminole and Creek rolls

Central Office (D.C.) Records:

M234   *Letters Received, Office of Indian Affairs, 1824–1881.* 962 rolls. DP. For an index, see M18, previously cited under general works treating all tribes (p. 258). For the actual letters, see

Roll 800: Seminole Agency [East], 1824–45 [closed 1836]

Rolls 806–97: Seminole Agency Emigration, 1827–59

Miscellaneous Records:

American State Papers: Documents Legislative and Executive of the Congress of the United States. 38 vols. Washington: Gales and Seaton, 1832–61. Particularly see Military Affairs Series, vol. 6: 450–781, for Seminole conflict with specific white families and individuals.

Removal Records:

[Manuscripts.] Miscellaneous Muster Rolls, 1832–46. 5 vols. and unbound papers. Entry 301, RG 75. Includes Seminole emigrants.[96]

School Records:

[Manuscripts.] Cashbook of J. E. Brecht, teacher and special disbursing agent, 1892–99. 31 ft. Held by National Archives–Southeast.

MISCELLANEOUS SOUTHEASTERN TRIBES

Central Office (D.C.) Records:

M234 *Letters Received, Office of Indian Affairs, 1824–1881.* 962 rolls. DP. For index, see M18, previously cited under general works treating all tribes (p. 258). For actual letters, see

Roll 2: Apalachicola Agency, 1826–42
Apalachicola Agency Reserves, 1841–42

Roll 29: Arkansas Superintendency, 1824–34

Rolls 266–89: Florida Superintendency, 1824–50

Rolls 290–91: Florida Superintendency Emigration, 1828–1853

Roll 291: Florida Superintendency Reserves, 1839–47

Factory Records:

M142 *Letterbook, Arkansas Trading House, 1805–1810.* 1 roll.

T1029 *Letterbook of the Natchitoches–Sulphur Fork Factory, 1809–1829.* 1 roll.

[Manuscripts.] Arkansas Factory Records. 5 vols. and ca. 1 in. of unbound papers. Entries 27–32, RG 75. Includes invoices, journals, ledgers, and a daybook; a letter book is filmed as M142, above.[97]

Removal Records:

[Manuscripts.] Miscellaneous Muster Rolls 1832–46. 5 vols. and unbound papers. Entry 301, RG 75. Includes Apalachicola emigrants, as well as others.[98]

Southern "bloodlines" boast a significant intermingling of races, and many modern families struggle to uncover the nonwhite heritage their ancestors sought to hide. It can be a formidable task. Yet it is one that *can* be accomplished, despite frustrating efforts in the commonly consulted federal records. Success requires the researcher to understand the unique cultures of Native American societies, the often knotty interweaving of American Indians with white and black contemporaries, and the inherent roadblocks created by random forces of nature. Those who seek out the less familiar resources cited in this handbook will earn rewards.

APPENDIXES

REFERENCE NOTES

1. The pertinent rolls are outlined in Part Two.

2. For background on post-removal records see Edward E. Hill, *Guide to Records in the National Archives of the United States Relating to American Indians* (Washington: National Archives and Records Service [NARS], 1981); Edward E. Hill, *Records of the Bureau of Indian Affairs*, Preliminary Inventory no. 163, 2 vols. (Washington: NARS, 1965); and *American Indians: A Select Catalog of National Archives Microfilm Publications*, 3d ed. (Washington: National Archives Trust Fund Board, 1998). The best federal repository for research on the Southeastern Indians is the National Archives's Southwest Region, in Fort Worth, Texas.

3. As examples: Eastern Cherokee Reservation in Swain County, North Carolina; Mississippi Choctaw Reservation in Neshoba County, Mississippi; Miccosukee [Seminole] Reservation in the Florida Everglades.

4. The common approach taken by genealogists—checking published government rolls—produces results in only a very small percentage of cases; but its occasional success deserves acknowledgment here. Amid turn-of-the-century effort to privatize tribal lands in Indian Territory, the U.S. created the Dawes Commission to establish "final rolls" for each of the Five Civilized Tribes. Concurrently, the Choctaw

and Cherokee nations prosecuted claims against the U.S. for benefits due under prior treaties. In the course of these proceedings, a wealth of genealogically valuable records were created by thousands of families outside Indian territory who had a knowledge or tradition of Indian ancestry and petitioned for acceptance. Whether or not they were successful, the oral accounts they gave of their ancestry can provide useful (though not necessarily reliable) clues. The Dawes Commission is discussed in more detail in chapter 4.

To identify those who appear on rolls of the Five Civilized Tribes, see National Archives micropublication M1186, *Enrollment Cards for the Five Civilized Tribes, 1898–1914*, which covers some 101,000 enrollees out of 250,000 applicants to the Dawes Commission. Extracted data from some 52,000 case files are available online at the National Archives website <http://www.nara.gov>. Bob Blankenship, *Cherokee Roots*; vol. 1, *Eastern Cherokee Rolls*; vol. 2, *Western Cherokee Rolls* (Cherokee, N. C.: Privately printed, 1992), indexes federal rolls from 1817 to 1924; and Blankenship, *Guion Miller Roll "Plus" of Eastern Cherokee East & West of Mississippi "1909"* (Cherokee, N. C.: Privately printed, ca. 1994), identifies rejected applicants as well as accepted ones. The Richard S. Lackey Collection at the McCain Library, University of Southern Mississippi, Hattiesburg, has a printed register of Choctaw claimants rejected by the Dawes Commission, entitled "Register of Members of Society Mississippi Choctaws: March 30, 1914."

An immense quantity of data that goes far beyond the details found in these rolls has been published for the Cherokee and Choctaw. For the Cherokee see Jerry Wright Jordan, *Cherokee by Blood: Records of Eastern Cherokee Ancestry in the U.S. Court of Claims, 1906–1910*, 9 vols. (Bowie, Md.: Heritage Books, 1987–97), with extracts from National Archives microfilm M685, *Records Relating to Enrollment of Eastern Cherokee by Guion Miller, 1908–10*. The Choctaw claims case does not provide the same type of turn-of-the-century oral history, but it is rich in records of the 1830s and 1840s relating to land locations and family relationships. See U. S. Court of Claims, *Choctaw Nation of Indians v. The United States*

(Washington: R. O. Polkinhorn[?], ca. 1882).

5. An excellent starting point for the historical study of Southeastern Indians is J. Leitch Wright, *The Only Land They Knew: The Tragic Story of the American Indians of the Old South* (New York: Free Press, 1981), and Grant Foreman, *The Five Civilized Tribes: Cherokee, Chickasaw, Choctaw, Creek, Seminole* (Norman: University of Oklahoma Press, 1934). Beyond this, Wright, *Creeks and Seminoles: The Destruction and Regeneration of the Muscogulge People* (Lincoln: University of Nebraska Press, 1986); Arrell M. Gibson, *The Chickasaws* (Norman: University of Oklahoma Press, 1971); Angie Debo, *The Rise and Fall of the Choctaw Republic* (Norman: University of Oklahoma Press, 1934); and John Ehle, *Trail of Tears: The Rise and Fall of the Cherokee Nation* (New York: Doubleday, 1988), provide a solid base for the five major Southeastern tribes.

6. For an overview of Southeastern miscegenation and racial attitudes, from a genealogical perspective, see Elizabeth Shown Mills, "Ethnicity and the Southern Genealogist: Myths and Misconceptions, Resources and Opportunities," in Robert M. Taylor Jr. and Ralph J. Crandall, *Generations and Change: Genealogical Perspectives in Social History* (Macon, Ga.: Mercer University Press, 1986), 89–110; and Gary B. Mills, "Tracing Free People of Color in the Antebellum South: Methods, Sources, and Perspectives," *National Genealogical Society Quarterly* 78 (December 1990): 262–78.

For a personal, historical perspective of a family's "secret shame" over Indian heritage and its efforts to obscure that ancestry, see General Thomas S. Woodward, *Woodward's Reminiscences of the Creek, or Muscogee Indians* (Montgomery, Ala.: Barrett & Wimbish, 1859), reissued as *The American Old West: Woodward's Reminiscences; A Personal Account of the Creek Nation in Georgia and Alabama* (Mobile: Southern University Press, 1965), particularly, 121–22, 124–26. Anyone with a tradition of Creek ancestry should also read Woodward for his genealogical data on many contemporary families.

7. This genealogical reconstruction of the Moniacs relies primarily on Gen. Woodward, who personally knew several generations of the

family; *Woodward's Reminiscences*, 78, 82. Woodward does not identify the Indian wife of Dixon Moniac; that identity is provided by Thomas McAdory Owen in *History of Alabama and Dictionary of Alabama Biography*, 4 vols. (1921; reprint, Spartanburg, S.C.: Reprint Co., 1978), 4: 1215. However, Owen relied heavily on another early Alabamian, Col. Albert J. Pickett, who lacked Woodward's advantage of personal acquaintance with these mixed-race families. Following Pickett, Owen identifies Charles Weatherford's wife as Sehoy *McGillivray*; Woodward, writing personally to Pickett in 1858, corrected Pickett on that point and recounted Sehoy's *McPherson* ancestry; *Woodward's Reminiscences*, 51–54.

8. Moniac's losses in this conflict totalled $12,595.25—including his home and furnishings, slaves, a cotton gin house, machinery, and livestock. For details, see *Letter from the Secretary of the Treasury . . . Relative to the Execution of an Act for the Relief of Samuel Menac, Passed 17th of April 1816* (Washington: Gales and Seaton, 1828), being House Doc. 200, 20th Cong., 1st Sess.

9. *Woodward's Reminiscences*, 82.

10. For the 1825 figures see Thos. L. McKenney to James Barbour, Secretary of War, 13 December 1825, *American State Papers: Documents Legislative and Executive of the Congress of the United States*, 32 vols. (Washington: Gales and Seaton, 1832–61), *Indian Affairs*, 2 vols., 2: 651. The 1828 census statistics are reported in the *Cherokee Phoenix*, 18 June 1828, p. 1.

11. Prominent examples of the multiracial harems of colonial Indian traders are provided by George Galphin of Silver Bluff on the Georgia–South Carolina border; John Leslie of Saint Augustine; and Zephaniah Kingsley of Fort George Island, Florida. Speaking of Galphin's colorblindness, Gen. Woodward reported: "Of the five varieties of the human family, [Galphin] raised children from three, and no doubt would have gone the whole hog, but the Malay and Mongol were out of his reach"; *Woodward's Reminiscences*, 91. Galphin's 1782 will is a testament to his lifestyle, acknowledging children by four women of three races and leaving 50£ sterling to "all . . . fatherless children within 30 miles of where

I live." See Abbeville County, South Carolina, probate box 40, pack 898, Clerk of Court's Office, Abbeville.

Instructive studies on black assimilation into Indian tribes are available as Daniel F. Littlefield Jr., *The Chickasaw Freedmen: A People Without a Country* (Westport, Conn.: Greenwood Press, 1980); and Littlefield, *Africans and Creeks: From the Colonial Period to the Civil War* (Westport: Greenwood Press, 1979). Wright, *Creeks and Seminoles*, also addresses the subject in depth.

12. Will Book B: 46, Greene County, Alabama. For the manumission of Tom and his purchase of his black family, see Deed Record A: 234, Greene County. Much additional material on the Toms—including one will not extant locally—appears in bundles 347 and 348, Papers Relating to Lands Located under Choctaw Treaty of 9/27/1830; box 819, Alabama—Huntsville Land Office, 1810–67, 1867–1905, Miscellaneous Records, 1833–54, 1879–92; in Record Group 49, Bureau of Land Management, National Archives.

13. Almon W. Lauber, *Indian Slavery in Colonial Times within the Present Limits of the United States* (New York: Columbia University, 1913), is the classic study of this aspect of history.

Southeastern Indians also practiced Indian slavery and used drastic measures to prevent runaways. The Chickasaw, for example, mutilated the feet of their Indian slaves by cutting sinews in the instep. Labor was still possible, flight was not. See Gibson, *Chickasaws*, 28–29.

14. For example, see the trail of court records and genealogical trees that resulted from the kidnapping of two Choctaw children at play—and their subsequent enslavement—by Henry Clay of Virginia in 1712, chronicled in Free Papers of Rachel Finley, Deed Book P: 270–76, Madison County, Alabama; *Fender [Finley] v. Marr*, Henry County, Virginia, Loose Papers, Determined Cases, 1788–1789, folder 66, Library of Virginia, Richmond; and in numerous other records on this family that appear in at least ten counties in Virginia, Tennessee, and Alabama.

15. Virginia Easley DeMarce, "'Verry Slitly Mixt': Tri-racial Isolate Families of the Upper South—A Genealogical Study," *National Genealogical Society Quarterly* 80 (March 1992): 5–35.

16. *Woodward's Reminiscences,* 19–20; Wright, *Only Land They Knew,* 9, 20, 227–8; Debo, *Rise and Fall of Choctaw Republic,* 15–18.

17. *Records of the Old Choctaw Trading House, 1803–1824,* NARA microfilm T500, roll 1. A published transcription exists as Ben Strickland, Jean Strickland, and P. N. Edwards, *Records of Choctaw Trading Post, St. Stephens, Mississippi Territory, 1803–1816,* 2 vols. (Moss Point, Miss.: Privately printed, 1984, 1990), see particularly 1: 7–11.

18. *American State Papers: Indian Affairs,* 2: 25.

19. For the land petition, see council journals, Colonial Office, 5/635: 67, Lockey Collection of British Records for East Florida, P. K. Yonge Library, University of Florida, Tallahassee. For the quotation, see Manuel Gayoso de Lemos to Baron de Carondelet, 13 September 1792, Spanish Provincial Archives, vol. 6, 1792–95, doc. 161 (MS, Mississippi State Department of Archives and History, Jackson). For Hardy's 1808 business, see Thomas Wright, Chickasaw agent, to Return J. Meigs, Cherokee agent, 2 May 1808, *Records of the Cherokee Agency in Tennessee, 1801–1835,* NARA microfilm M208, roll 4. For the Choctaw Perrys, see *Choctaw Nation vs. U.S.,* especially p. 172.

20. "Report on the Petition of the half-breeds resident on Alabama [River], sufferers by the civil war among the Creek," 1 January 1816, *Letters Received by the Secretary of War Relating to Indian Affairs, 1800–1823,* NARA microfilm M271, roll 1, frames 1103–7; Ward's Register, Division 3, pp. 67–71, dated 24 August 1831, in *Choctaw Nation vs. U. S.; Woodward's Reminiscences,* 98.

For the most reliable account of Rachel's McGillivray ancestry, see *Woodward's Reminiscences,* 53–57, 98. Her father, Durant, is said by Benjamin Hawkins, a contemporary who was a longtime U.S. agent to the Creek, to have been "a little mixed with African blood." See Benjamin Hawkins, *Letters of Benjamin Hawkins, 1796–1806,* Collections of the Georgia Historical Society, vol. 9 (Savannah: Morning News, 1916), 43.

21. For details of the land allotment, see Charles J. Kappler, comp. and ed., *Indian Affairs: Laws and Treaties,* 2 vols. (Washington: Government Printing Office, 1904): 2: 310–19. See also Mary Elizabeth Young,

Redskins, Ruffleshirts, and Rednecks: Indian Allotments in Alabama and Mississippi, 1830–1860 (Norman: University of Oklahoma Press, 1961); and Theda Purdue, "Indians in Southern History," in Frederick E. Hoxie, ed., *Indians in American History* (Arlington Heights, Ill.: Harlan Davidson, 1988), 146–48.

22. John R. Swanton, *Source Material for the Social and Ceremonial Life of the Choctaw Indians*, Bulletin 103, Smithsonian Institution, Bureau of American Ethnology (Washington: Government Printing Office, 1931), 120–21; and Debo, *Choctaw Republic*, 17.

23. A valuable introduction to these lesser-known tribes is provided by John R. Swanton's *The Indian Tribes of North America*, Bureau of American Ethnology Bulletin 145 (1952; reprinted, Washington: Smithsonian Institution Press, 1969).

24. Gibson, *The Chickasaws*, 6; Wright, *Creeks and Seminoles*, 13–14.

25. For major trading families, see Wright, *Only Land They Knew*, 110. For the Creek trade specifically, see Kathryn E. Holland Braund, *Deerskins & Duffels: Creek Indian Trade with Anglo-America, 1685–1815* (Lincoln: University of Nebraska Press, 1993).

26. As a beginning point for locating records of these families, see Mary McCampbell Bell, Clifford Dwyer, and William Abbott Henderson, "Finding Manuscript Collections: NUCMC, NIDS, and RLIN," *National Genealogical Society Quarterly* 77 (December 1989): 208–18.

27. William L. McDowell Jr., ed., *Journals of the Commissioners of the Indian Trade; September 20, 1710–August 29, 1718* (1955; reprint, Columbia: South Carolina Department of Archives and History [SCDAH], 1992); McDowell, ed., *Documents Relating to Indian Affairs, May 21, 1750–August 7, 1754* (1958; reprinted, Columbia, SCDAH, 1992); and McDowell, ed., *Documents Relating to Indian Affairs, 1754–1765* (1970; reprinted, Columbia: SCDAH, 1992).

28. McDowell, *Journals of the Commissioners*, 3–4.

29. McDowell, *Documents Relating to Indian Affairs, 1764–1756*, 297–99.

30. Ibid., 497–99.

31. Bill Barron, *The Vaudreuil Papers: A Calendar and Index of the*

Personal and Private Records of Pierre de Regaud de Vaudreuil, Royal Governor of the French Province of Louisiana, 1743–53 (New Orleans: Polyanthos, 1975), citing manuscript vol. 1:10 verso.

32. Ibid., 368, 372, citing manuscript vol. 3: 159, 166.

33. Ibid., 65, citing LO 200, 1749.

34. Ibid., 142, citing LO 410.

35. Ibid., 2, citing LO 19, 1743.

36. Even among the Cherokee, writing was only a nineteenth-century phenomenon. The Cherokee alphabet was invented in 1809 by Sequoia, aka George Guest (Gist).

37. For overviews of each tribe, see Clark Wissler, *Indians of the United States*, rev. ed., Lucy Wales Kluckhorn, ed. (Garden City, N.Y.: Anchor Books, 1966); and Swanton, *Indian Tribes of North America*.

38. For the Indians of Louisiana, a starting point would be Fred B. Kniffen, Hiram F. Gregory, and George A. Stokes, *The Historic Indian Tribes of Louisiana, from 1542 to the Present* (Baton Rouge: Louisiana State University Press, 1987). Other major works include F. Todd Smith, *The Caddo Indians: Tribes at the Convergence of Empires, 1542–1854* (College Station: Texas A & M University Press, 1995); and Cecile Elkins Carter, *Caddo Indians: Where We Come From* (Norman: University of Oklahoma Press, 1995).

39. Hill, *Guide . . . Relating to American Indians*, 5–13, 24–25.

40. For extensive background, see Laurence F. Schmeckebier, *The Office of Indian Affairs: Its History, Activities, and Organization* (1927; reprint, New York: AMS Press, 1972).

41. Secondarily, many supporting records are scattered in other departments and divisions of the government—principally the Bureau of Land Management, the Court of Claims, the Fish and Wildlife Service, the Geological Survey, the State Department, the Supreme Court, and the Treasury Department. See figure 8.

42. Howard H. Wehmann and Benjamin L. DeWhitt, *A Guide to Pre-Federal Records in the National Archives* (Washington: NARA, 1989), 129; Edward E. Hill, *The Office of Indian Affairs, 1824–1880: Historical Sketches* (New York: Clearwater Press, 1974).

43. Hill, *Guide to Records in the National Archives . . . Relating to American Indians*, 17–23, concisely surveys the factory system.

44. Ibid. For specifics of treaties between the United States and the various Indian nations, see Kappler, *Indian Affairs*.

45. Hill, *Guide to Records in the National Archives . . . Relating to American Indians*, 67, 69–74. Hill, *Records of the Bureau of Indian Affairs*, 1: 69–71. Many federal records relating to removal of the Five Civilized Tribes have been published in the Congressional Serial Set. See Steven L. Johnson, *Guide to American Indian Documents in the Congressional Serial Set: 1817–1899* (New York: Clearwater Publishing Co., 1974). For background on the removals and reserves, see Grant Foreman, *Indian Removal: The Emigration of the Five Civilized Tribes of Indians* (Norman: University of Oklahoma Press, 1932); and Mary Elizabeth Young, *Redskins, Ruffleshirts, and Redneck*. For the Eastern Cherokee who did not remove, see John R. Finger, *The Eastern Band of Cherokees, 1819–1900* (Knoxville: University of Tennessee Press, 1984).

46. Anne Bruner Eales and Robert M. Kvasnicka, *Guide to Genealogical Research in the National Archives*, 3d ed. (Washington: National Archives Trust Fund Board, 2000), 218. See also Kent Carter, *The Dawes Commission and the Allotment of the Five Civilized Tribes, 1893–1914* (Orem, Utah: Ancestry, 1999); and D. S. Otis, *The Dawes Act and the Allotment of Indian Land*, The Civilization of the American Indian Series, vol. 123 (Norman: University of Oklahoma Press, 1975).

47. *American Indians: A Select Catalog of National Archives Microfilm Publications*, 43.

48. Hill, *Records of the Bureau of Indian Affairs*, 1: 150–51.

49. Hill, *Guide to Records in the National Archives . . . Relating to American Indians*, 94–95.

50. *American Indians: A Select Catalog*, 14; Hill, *Records of the Bureau of Indian Affairs*, 1: 44.

51. Also valuable for both background perspective and record descriptions of the Five Civilized Tribes in particular is Curt B. Witcher and George J. Nixon, "Tracking Native American Family History," in Loretto Dennis Szucs and Sandra Hargreaves Luebking, eds. *The Source:*

A Guidebook of American Genealogy, rev. ed. (Salt Lake City: Ancestry, 1997), 521–72. Also see Kent Carter, "Wantabes and Outalucks: Searching for Indian Ancestors in Federal Records," *Chronicles of Oklahoma* 66 (Spring 1988): 99–104; Carter, "Deciding Who Can Be Cherokee: Enrollment Records of the Dawes Commission," *Chronicles of Oklahoma* 69 (Summer 1991): 174–205; Carter, "Federal Indian Policy: The Dawes Commission, 1887–1898," *Prologue* 22 (Winter 1990): 339–49; Carter, "Federal Indian Policy: Cherokee Enrollment, 1891–1907," *Prologue* 23 (Spring 1991): 25–38; and Carter, "Snakes and Scribes: The Dawes Commission and the Enrollment of the Creeks," *Prologue* 29 (Spring 1997): 28–41.

52. Product Sales Section (NWPS), National Archives and Records Administration; 700 Pennsylvania Avenue, NW; Washington, DC 20408. The parent facility of the National Archives is located at this same address. The Southeast facility is located at 1557 St. Joseph Avenue; East Point, GA 30344-2593; the Southwest facility is located at 501 West Felix Street, Bldg. 1, Dock 1; Fort Worth, TX 76115.

53. See also Wehmann and DeWhitt, *Guide to Pre-Federal Records*, 129–41.

54. Hill, *Records of the Bureau of Indian Affairs*, 1: 34–35.

55. Searchable database versions of the Dawes Commission's enrollment cards are also available. For NARA's free database, see its website <http:/www.nara.gov/nara/nail.html>. For a commercial database, see *Native American Collection*, CD-ROM (Orem, Utah: Genref, 1997).

56. Hill, *Records of the Bureau of Indian Affairs*, 1: 14–31.

57. Described in ibid., 2: 304–8.

58. For abstracts, see the nine volumes of Jordan, *Cherokee by Blood*.

59. T529 is also available in printed form as *The Final Rolls of Citizens and Freedmen of the Five Civilized Tribes in Indian Territory*, 5 vols. (Washington: Government Printing Office, 1907); see also *Index to the Final Rolls of Citizens and Freedmen of the Five Civilized Tribes in Indian Territory* (Washington: Government Printing Office, 1907).

60. Described in Gaiselle Kerner, *Records of the United States Court of Claims*, Preliminary Inventories no. 58 (Washington: NARS, 1953), 8–

16. See also Blankenship, *Cherokee Roots*, and Blankenship, *Guion Miller Roll "Plus,"* both previously cited.

61. Described in Hill, *Records of the Bureau of Indian Affairs*, 1: 196.

62. Described in Hill, ibid., 1: 75. The Siler Roll is published as David W. Siler, *The Eastern Cherokee: A Census of the Cherokee Nation in North Carolina, Tennessee, Alabama, and Georgia in 1851* (Cottonport, La.: Polyanthos, 1972).

63. Described in Szucs and Luebking, *The Archives . . . National Archives Field Branches*, 185.

64. Described in Hill, *Records of the Bureau of Indian Affairs*, 1: 168–72.

65. Described in ibid., 1: 24.

66. Described in ibid., 1: 253.

67. Described in ibid., 1: 74–82. See also Jack D. Baker, *Cherokee Emigration Rolls, 1817–1835* (Oklahoma City: Baker Publishing Co., 1977).

68. Described in Hill, *Records of the Bureau of Indian Affairs*, 1: 77.

69. Described in ibid., 1: 162.

70. Described in ibid., 1: 180.

71. Described in ibid., 2: 309.

72. Described in ibid., 1: 83.

73. Described in ibid., 1: 25.

74. Described in Daniel T. Goggin and H. Stephen Helton, *General Records of the Department of State*, Preliminary Inventories no. 157, (Washington: NARS, 1963), 69.

75. Described in Hill, *Records of the Bureau of Indian Affairs*, 1: 30–31.

76. Described in ibid., 1: 82–83.

77. Described in ibid., 1: 83.

78. Described in ibid., 2: 309.

79. Described in ibid., 1: 83–84. The Armstrong Roll is published as William Ward's Register in *Mississippi Genealogical Exchange* 18 (Spring 1972): 11–14. An 1837 Choctaw Indian muster roll also exists as microfilm publication 260 at the Alabama Department of Archives and History, Montgomery.

80. Described in Hill, *Records of the Bureau of Indian Affairs*, 1: 173. See also Kent Carter, *Records of the Bureau of Indian Affairs: Records of the Five Civilized Tribes; Agency Records Relating to the Identification of Mississippi Choctaws, 1899–1904*, Microcopy 7RA116, 2 rolls, a special publication of the NARA's Southwest Region, Fort Worth.

81. Described in Edward E. Hill and Renee Jaussaud, comps., *Inventory of the Records of the Department of the Interior*, Inventory no. 13 (Washington: NARA, 1987), entry 715.

82. Described in Hill, *Records of the Bureau of Indian Affairs*, 1: 25. See also Strickland, Strickland, and Edwards, *Records of Choctaw Trading Post*, previously cited.

83. Described in Hill, *Records of the Bureau of Indian Affairs*, 1: 84.

84. Described in Harry P. Yoshpe and Philip P. Brower, *Preliminary Inventory of the Land-Entry Papers of the General Land Office*, Preliminary Inventories no. 22 (Washington: NARS, 1949), 10.

85. Described in ibid., 15

86. Described in ibid., 45. Szucs and Luebking, *The Archives . . . National Archives Field Branches*, 233, catalogs these records amid the holdings of the NARA's Southeast Region, Atlanta.

87. Described in Hill, *Records of the Bureau of Indian Affairs*, 1: 84–88. See also the [John] Claiborne Commission Papers, at the University of North Carolina, Chapel Hill.

88. Described in Hill, *Records of the Bureau of Indian Affairs*, 1: 150–54. See also *Choctaw Nation vs. U. S.* An index is available as *A Complete Roll of All Choctaw Claimants and Their Heirs*, Joe R. Goss, ed. (Conway, Ark.: Oldbuck Press, ca. 1992).

89. This document is published, with an index, as *The Choctaw Academy: Official Correspondence, 1825–1941*, Joe R. Goss, ed. (Conway, Ark.: Oldbuck Press, n.d.). For related background, see Clara Sue Kidwell, *Choctaws and Missionaries in Mississippi, 1818–1918* (Norman: University of Oklahoma Press, 1995).

90. Described in Hill, *Records of the Bureau of Indian Affairs*, 2: 311–12.

91. Described in ibid., 1: 26–27. See also Hawkins, *Letters of Benjamin*

Hawkins, 43.

92. Described in Hill, *Records of the Bureau of Indian Affairs*, 1: 88, 91.

93. Described in ibid., 1: 88–91.

94. Described in ibid., 1: 162.

95. Described in Yoshpe and Brower, *Preliminary Inventory of the Land-Entry Papers*, 15. Szucs and Luebking, *The Archives . . . National Archives Field Branches*, 230, catalogs these records amid the holdings of the NARA's Southeast Region, Atlanta.

96. Described in Hill, *Records of the Bureau of Indian Affairs*, 1: 91.

97. Described in ibid., 1: 23–24.

98. Described in ibid., 1: 91.

FURTHER STUDY:
A SELECTIVE BIBLIOGRAPHY

NOTE

The works that follow provide a wealth of additional avenues to explore. Some present cultural and historical context; others represent contemporary memoirs; and many present abstracted, transcribed, or compiled records. After the initial section, which surveys archival guides and general literature that crosses tribal bounds, the bibliography focuses upon each of the Five Civilized Tribes. A final "Miscellaneous" section covers valuable publications for many of the smaller tribes that have peopled the American Southeast.

GENERAL:
ARCHIVAL GUIDES & BIBLIOGRAPHIES

A *Dictionary Catalog of the Edward E. Ayer Collection of Americana and American Indians in the Newberry Library.* 16 vols., 2 supplements. Chicago: Newberry Library, 1961–80.

American Indians: A Select Catalog of National Archives Microfilm Publication. Washington: National Archives Trust Fund Board, 1993.

American State Papers: Documents Legislative and Executive of the Congress of the United States. 38 vols. Washington: Gales and Seaton, 1832–61. (Materials on Indians and Indian-white interaction are scattered throughout, particularly in the Indian Affairs, Military Affairs, and Public Land series.)

Anderson, William L., and Frances G. Davenport. *Guide to the Manuscript Materials for the History of the United States to 1783, in the British Museum, in the Minor London Archives, and in the Libraries of Oxford and Cambridge*. Washington: Carnegie Institution, 1908.

Andrews, Charles M. *Guide to Materials for American History, to 1783, in the Public Record Office of Great Britain*. 2 vols. Washington: Carnegie Institution, 1912–14.

Archivo Nacional de Cuba. *Catálogo de los fondos de las Floridas*. Havana: A Muniz y hermano, 1944.

Astorquia, Madeline Ulane Bonnel, et al. *Guide des sources de l'histoire des États-Unis dans les archives françaises*. Paris: France Expansion, 1976.

Barron, Bill. *The Vaudreuil Papers: A Calendar and Index of the Personal and Private Records of Pierre de Regaud de Vaudreuil, Royal Governor of the French Province of Louisiana, 1743–53*. New Orleans: Polyanthos, 1975.

Beers, Henry Putney. *The French in North America: A Bibliographical Guide to French Archives, Reproductions, and Research Missions*. Baton Rouge: Louisiana State University Press, 1957.

Bell, Herbert C., David W. Parker, et al. *Guide to British West Indian Archive Materials, in London and in the Islands, for the History of the United States*. Washington: Carnegie Institution, 1926.

Bermudez Plata, Cristobal. *El Archivo General de Indias de Sevilla, sede del Americanismo*. Madrid: N.p., 1951.

Carter, Kent. *Records of the Bureau of Indian Affairs: Records of the Five Civilized Tribes; Agency Records Relating to the Identification of Mississippi Choctaws, 1899–1904*. Microcopy 7RA116, 2 rolls. Fort Worth: National Archives—Southwest Region, n.d.

Catalog of the P. K. Yonge Library of Florida History. 4 vols. Boston: G. K. Hall and Co., 1977.

Chepesiuk, Ron, and Arnold Shankman. *American Indian Archival Material: A Guide to Holdings in the Southeast*. Westport, Conn.: Greenwood Press, 1982.

Conrad, Glenn R., and Carl A. Brasseaux. *A Selected Bibliography of*

Scholarly Literature on Colonial Louisiana and New France. Lafayette: Center for Louisiana Studies, 1982.

Cuba. *Documents Pertaining to the Floridas Which Are Kept in Different Archives of Cuba, Appendix no. 1: Official List of Documentary Funds of the Floridas—Now Territories of the States of Louisiana, Alabama, Mississippi, Georgia, and Florida—Kept in the National Archives*. Havana: N.p., 1945.

Davis, Robert Scott. *A Guide to Native American (Indian) Research Sources at the Georgia Department of Archives and History*. Jasper, Ga.: privately printed, 1985.

Daythal, Kendall. *A Supplement to A Guide to Manuscripts Relating to the American Indian in the Library of the American Philosophical Society*. Philadelphia: American Philosophical Society, 1982.

Eales, Anne Bruner, and Robert M. Kvasnicka. *Guide to Genealogical Research in the National Archives*. 3d ed. Washington: National Archives Trust Fund Board, 2000.

Fogelson, Raymond D. *The Cherokees: A Critical Bibliography*. Bibliographical Series, Newberry Library Center for the History of the American Indian. Bloomington: Indiana University Press, 1978.

Freeman, John F. *A Guide to Manuscripts Relating to the American Indian in the Library of the American Philosophical Society*. Philadelphia: American Philosophical Society, 1966.

Goggan, Daniel T., and H. Stephen Helton. *General Records of the Department of State*. Preliminary Inventories no. 157. Washington: National Archives and Records Service, 1963.

Griffen, William B. *A Calendar of Spanish Records Relating to Florida, 1512–1790*. Saint Augustine: William B. Griffen, 1959.

Griffin, Grace Gardner. *A Guide to Manuscripts Relating to American History in British Depositories, Reproduced from the Division of Manuscripts of the Library of Congress*. Washington: Library of Congress, 1946.

Guía de fuentes para la historia de Ibero–América conservados en España. Madrid: Dirección General de Archivos y Bibliotecas, 1965, 1969.

Haggard, J. Villasaña. *Handbook for Translators of Spanish Historical Documents*. Austin: University of Texas, 1941.

Harper, Josephine L. *Guide to the Draper Manuscripts*. Madison: State Historical Society of Wisconsin, 1983.

Hill, Edward E. *Guide to Records in the National Archives of the United States Relating to American Indians*. Washington: National Archives and Records Service, 1981.

———. *The Office of Indian Affairs, 1824–1880: Historical Sketches*. New York: Clearwater Press, 1974.

———. *Records of the Bureau of Indian Affairs*. Preliminary Inventory no. 163. 2 vols. Washington: National Archives and Records Service, 1965.

——— and Renee Jaussaud. *Inventory of the Records of the Department of the Interior*. Inventory no. 13. Washington: National Archives and Records Administration, 1987.

Hill, Roscoe R. *Descriptive Catalogue of the Documents Relating to the History of the United States in the Papeles Procedentes de Cuba, Deposited in the Archivo General de Indias at Seville*. Washington: Carnegie Institution, 1916.

Johnson, Steven L. *Guide to American Indian Documents in the Congressional Serial Set, 1817–1899*. Bethesda, Md: Congressional Information Services, 2000.

Kelsay, Laura E. *Cartographic Records of the Bureau of Indian Affairs*. National Archives and Records Service, Special List no. 13. Washington: Government Printing Office, 1977.

Kerner, Gaiselle. *Records of the United States Court of Claims*. Preliminary Inventories no. 58. Washington: National Archives and Records Service, 1953.

Manucy, Albert C. "Florida History (1650–1750) in the Spanish Records of North Carolina State Department of Archives and History." *Florida Historical Quarterly* 25 (1947): 319–32.

Mills, Elizabeth Shown. "Spanish Records: Locating Anglo and Latin Ancestry in the Colonial Southeast." *National Genealogical Society Quarterly* 73 (1985): 243–61.

Parker, David W. *Guide to the Materials for United States History in Canadian Archives*. Washington: Carnegie Institution, 1913.

Paullin, Charles O., and Frederic L. Paxson. *Guide to Materials in London Archives for the History of the United States since 1783*. Washington: Carnegie Institution, 1914.

Pas, Julián. *Catálogo de manuscritos de América existentes en la Biblioteca Nacional*. Madrid: Tip. de Archivos, 1933.

Platt, Lyman D. *Una guía genealógica-histórica de Latinoamerica*. Ramona, Calif.: Acoma Books, 1978.

Prucha, Francis P. *A Bibliographical Guide to the History of Indian-White Relations in the United States*. Chicago: University of Chicago, 1977.

Robertson, James Alexander. *List of Documents in Spanish Archives Relating to the History of the United States Which Have Been Printed or of Which Transcripts Are Preserved in American Libraries*. Washington: Carnegie Institution, 1910.

Serrano y Sanz, Manuel. *Documentos históricos de la Florida y la Luisiana, siglos XVI y XVIII*. Madrid: Suarez, 1912.

Shepherd, William. *Guide to the Materials for the United States in Spanish Archives (Simancas, the Archivo Histórico Nacional, and Seville)*. Washington: Carnegie Institution, 1907.

Spindel, Donna. *Introductory Guide to Indian-Related Records (to 1876) in the North Carolina State Archives*. Raleigh: North Carolina Division of Archives and History, 1977.

Steck, Francis B. *A Tentative Guide to Historic Materials on the Spanish Borderlands*. Philadelphia: Catholic Historical Society of Philadelphia, 1943.

Sturgill, Claude C. *Guide to the British Collection in the P. K. Yonge Library of Florida History*. Gainesville: University of Florida, n.d.

Szucs, Loretto Dennis, and Sandra Hargreaves Luebking. *The Archives: A Guide to the National Archives Field Branches*. Salt Lake City: Ancestry, 1988.

Tornero Tinajero, Pablo. *Relaciones de dependencia entre Florida y Estados Unidos, 1783–1820*. Madrid: Ministerio de Asuntos Exteriores, 1979.

Tudela de la Orden, José. *Los manuscritos de América en las bibliotecas de España*. Madrid: Ediciones Cultura Hispanica, 1954.

Wehmann, Howard H., and Benjamin L. DeWhitt. *A Guide to Pre-Federal Records in the National Archives*. Washington: National Archives and Records Administration, 1989.

Works Progress Administration, North Carolina. *List of Papeles Procedentes de Cuba (Cuban Papers) in the Archives of the North Carolina Historical Commission*. Raleigh: North Carolina Historic Records Survey, 1942.

Yoshpe, Harry P., and Philip P. Brower. *Preliminary Inventory of the Land-Entry Papers of the General Land Office*. Preliminary Inventories no. 22. Washington: National Archives and Records Service, 1949.

GENERAL:
HISTORIES, MEMOIRS & RECORD ABSTRACTS

Abel, Annie Heloise. *The American Indian as Slaveholder and Secessionist*. 1919. Reprint, Lincoln: University of Nebraska Press, 1992.

Adair, James. *The History of the American Indians: Particularly Those Adjoining to the Mississippi, East and West Florida, Georgia, South and North Carolina, and Virginia, 1775*. 1768. Reprint, New York: Johnson Reprint Co., 1966.

Alden, John Richard. *John Stuart and the Southern Colonial Frontier: A Study of Indian Relations, War, Trade and Land Problems in the Southern Wilderness, 1754–1775*. 1944. Reprint, New York: Gordian Press, 1966.

Axtell, James. *The Indians' New South: Cultural Change in the Colonial Southeast*. Baton Rouge: Louisiana State University Press, 1997.

Bierer, Bert W. *Indians and Artifacts in the Southeast*. Columbia, S.C.: Privately printed, 1980.

Bonney, Rachel A., and J. Anthony Paredes. *Anthropologists and Indians in the New South*. Tuscaloosa: University of Alabama Press, 2001.

Bureau of American Ethnology. *Bulletins*. Washington: Smithsonian Institution, ongoing series. (This massive collection, found in government documents repositories nationwide, is far too extensive to itemize in the present bibliography. Many of its book-length works by Albert S. Gatschet, John R. Swanton, and others are being reprinted by other presses and are individually cited herein.)

Bushnell, David I. *Native Cemeteries and Forms of Burial East of the Mississippi*. Washington: Government Printing Office, 1920.

————. *Native Villages and Village Sites East of the Mississippi.* Washington: Government Printing Office, 1919.

————. *Tribal Migrations East of the Mississippi.* Washington: Smithsonian Institute, 1934.

Calendar of the Frontier Wars Papers of the Draper Collection of Manuscripts. Publications of the State Historical Society of Wisconsin, Calendar Series, vol. 6. Utica, Ky.: McDowell Publications, 1991.

Calendar of the Kentucky Papers of the Draper Collection of Manuscripts. Publications of the State Historical Society of Wisconsin, Calendar Series, vol. 2. Mabel Clare Weakes, ed. Madison: The Society, 1925.

Calendar of the Tennessee and King's Mountain Papers of the Draper Collection of Manuscripts. Publications of the State Historical Society of Wisconsin, Calendar Series, vol. 3, Joseph Schafer, superintendent. Madison: The Society, 1929.

Calendar of the Thomas Sumpter Papers of the Draper Collection of Manuscripts. Publications of the State Historical Society of Wisconsin, Calendar Series, vol. 5. Utica, Ky., McDowell Publications, 1991.

Carter, Kent. *The Dawes Commission and the Allotment of the Five Civilized Tribes, 1893–1914.* Orem, Utah: Ancestry, 1999.

————. "Federal Indian Policy: The Dawes Commission, 1887–1898." *Prologue* 22 (1990): 339–49.

————. "Wantabes and Outalucks: Searching for Indian Ancestors in Federal Records." *Chronicles of Oklahoma* 66 (1988): 99–104

Cayton, Andrew R. L. and Frederika J. Teute, ed. *Contact Points: American Frontiers from the Mohawk Valley to the Mississippi, 1750–1830.* Chapel Hill: University of North Carolina Press, 1998.

Coker, William S., and Thomas D. Watson. *Indian Traders of the Southeastern Spanish Borderlands: Panton, Leslie & Company and John Forbes & Company, 1783–1847.* Pensacola: University of West Florida, 1986.

Confederation of American Indians. *Indian Reservations: A State and Federal Handbook.* Jefferson, N. C.: McFarland and Co., 1986.

Connor, Jeannette M. *Colonial Records of Spanish Florida; Letters and Reports of Governors and Secular Persons.* Deland: Florida State Historical Society, 1925.

Corkran, David H. *The Carolina Indian Frontier.* Columbia: University of South Carolina Press for the S. C. Tercentennial Commission, 1970.

Cotteril, Robert Spencer. *The Southern Indians: The Story of the Civilized Tribes before Removal.* Norman: University of Oklahoma Press, 1954.

Crane, Verner W. *The Southern Frontier, 1670–1732.* 1929. Reprint, New York: Norton, 1981.

Daunton, Martin, and Rick Halpern, eds. *Empire and Others: British Encounters with Indigenous Peoples, 1600–1850.* Durham: Duke University Press, 1999.

De la Peña y Camara, José; Ernest J. Burrus; et al. *Catalogo de documentos del Archivo General de Indias, Sección V, Gobierno, Audiencia de Santo Domingo, sobre la epoca Española de Luisiana.* 2 vols. New Orleans and Madrid: Loyala University, 1968.

DeMarce, Virginia Easley. "'Very Slittly Mixt': Tri-racial Isolate Families of the Upper South—A Genealogical Study. *National Genealogical Society Quarterly* 80 (1992): 5–35.

————. "Looking at Legends—Lumbee and Melungeon: Applied Genealogy and the Origins of Tri-racial Isolate Settlements." *National Genealogical Society Quarterly* 81 (1993): 24–45.

DeVorsey, Louis, Jr. "Indian Boundaries in Colonial Georgia." *Georgia Historical Quarterly* 54 (1970): 63–78.

————. *The Indian Boundary in the Southern Colonies, 1763–1775.* Chapel Hill: University of North Carolina Press, 1966.

Final Rolls of Citizens and Freedmen of the Five Civilized Tribes in Indian Territory. 5 vols. Washington: Government Printing Office, 1907. (See also *Index to the Final Rolls . . . ,* listed below.)

Foreman, Grant. *Advancing the Frontier, 1830–1860.* Norman: University of Oklahoma Press, 1933.

————. *The Five Civilized Tribes: A Brief History and a Century of Progress.* Reprinted. Norman: University of Oklahoma Press, 1966.

————. *The Five Civilized Tribes: Cherokee, Chickasaw, Choctaw, Creek, Seminole.* Norman: University of Oklahoma Press, 1934.

————. *Indian Removal: The Emigration of the Five Civilized Tribes of Indians.* Norman: University of Oklahoma Press, 1953.

Foster, Laurence. *Negro-Indian Relationships in the Southeast.* 1935. Reprint, New York: AMS Press, 1978.

Fundaburk, Emma Lila. *Southeastern Indians: Life Portraits; A Catalogue of Pictures, 1564–1860.* Luverne, Ala.: Privately printed, 1958.

Gallaher, Ruth A. "The Indian Agent in the United States Before 1850." *Iowa Journal of History and Politics* 14 (1916): 3–32.

Galloway, Colin G. *The American Revolution in Indian Country: Crisis and Diversity in Native American Communities.* New York: Cambridge University Press, 1995.

Gatschet, Albert. *"Real," "True," or "Genuine" in Indian Languages.* New York: G. P. Putnam's Sons, 1899.

Gilbert, William Harlen. *Memorandum Concerning the Characteristics of the Larger Mixed-Blood Racial Islands of the Eastern United States.* Chapel Hill [?]: Privately printed [?], 1946.

———. *Surviving Indian Groups of the Eastern United States.* Washington: Government Printing Office, 1949.

Heinegg, Paul. *Free African Americans of North Carolina, Virginia, and South Carolina from the Colonial Period to about 1820.* 4th ed. 2 vols. Baltimore: Clearfield Co., 2001.

———. *Free African Americans of Maryland and Delaware from the Colonial Period to 1810.* Baltimore: Clearfield Co., 2000.

Hodgson, Adam. *Remarks during a Journey through North America in the Years 1819, 1820, and 1821 in a Series of Letters; With an Appendix, Containing an Account of Several of the Indian Tribes and the Principal Missionary Stations, &c.* ca. 1823–24. Reprint, Westport, Conn.: Negro Universities Press, 1970.

Holmes, Jack D. L. *Documentos inéditos para la historia de la Luisiana (1792–1810).* Madrid: J. Porrua Turanzas, 1963.

Hoxie, Frederick E. *Indians in American History.* Arlington Heights, Ill.: Harlan Davidson, 1988.

———, Ronald Hoffman, and Peter J. Albert, eds. *Native Americans and the Early Republic.* Charlottesville: University of Virginia Press, ca. 1999.

Hudson, Charles and Carmen Chaves Tesser, eds. *The Forgotten Centuries: Indians and Europeans in the American South, 1521–1704.* Athens: University of Georgia, 1994.

Index to the Final Rolls of Citizens and Freedmen of the Five Civilized Tribes in Indian Territory. Washington: Government Printing Office, 1907. (See also *Final Rolls . . .* above.)

Jackson, Curtis E., and Marcia J. Galli. *A History of the Bureau of Indian Affairs and Its Activities among Indians.* San Francisco: R & E Research Associates, 1977.

Jones, Charles Colcock. *Antiquities of the Southern Indians, Particularly of the Georgia Tribes*. 1873. Reprint, New York: AMS Press for Peabody Museum of Archaeology and Ethnology, 1973.

Jones, Dorothy V. *License for Empire: Colonialism by Treaty in Early America*. Chicago: University of Chicago Press, 1982.

Kappler, Charles J., comp. and ed. *Indian Affairs: Laws and Treaties*. 2 vols. Washington: Government Printing Office, 1904.

Kinnaird, Lawrence. *Spain in the Mississippi Valley, 1765–1794*, vols. 2–4 of *Annual Report of the American Historical Association for the Year 1945*. 4 vols. Washington: Government Printing Office, 1946.

Lauber, Almon W. *Indian Slavery in Colonial Times within the Present Limits of the United States*. New York: Columbia Press, 1913.

Linton, Ralph, ed. *Acculturation in Seven American Indian Tribes*. New York: D. Appleton–Century Co., 1940.

Lockey, Joseph B., comp., *East Florida, 1783–1785: A File of Documents Assembled and Many of Them Translated by Joseph Byrne Lockey*. Berkeley: University of California, 1949.

McDowell, William L., Jr., ed. *Documents Relating to Indian Affairs, 21 May 1750–August 7, 1754*. 1958. Reprint, Columbia, S.C. Department of Archives and History, 1992.

———. *Documents Relating to Indian Affairs, 1754–1765*. 1970. Reprint, Columbia: S. C. Department of Archives and History, 1992.

———. *Journals of the Commissioners of the Indian Trade, September 20, 1710–August 29, 1718*. 1955. Reprint, Columbia: S. C. Department of Archives and History, 1992.

McKenney, Thomas L. *Reports and Proceedings of Col. McKenney, on the Subject of His Recent Tour among the Southern Indians, as Submitted to Congress with the Message of the President*. Washington: Gales and Seaton, 1828.

——— and James T. Hall. *History of the Indian Tribes of North America, with Biographical Sketches and Anecdotes of the Principal Chiefs*. 1836. Reprint, St. Clair Shores, Mich.: Scholarly Press, 1977.

McLoughlin, William G. "Red Indians, Black Slavery, and White Racism: America's Slaveholding Indians." *American Quarterly* 26 (1974): 367–85.

Mereness, Newton Dennison, ed. *Travels in the American Colonies*. New York: Macmillan Co., 1916.

Mississippi Writer's Project, Work Projects Administration. *Spanish Provincial Archives, 1759–1806*. Microfilm, 4 rolls. Jackson: Mississippi Department of Archives and History, n.d.

Nash, Gary B. "The Image of the Indians in the Southern Colonial Mind." *William and Mary Quarterly*. 3rd series 29 (1972): 197–230.

Otis, D. S. *The Dawes Act and the Allotment of Indian Land*. The Civilization of the American Indian Series, vol. 123. Norman: University of Oklahoma Press, 1975.

Owsley, Frank L. Jr. *Struggles for the Gulf Borderlands: The Creek War and the Battle of New Orleans, 1812–1815*. 1981. Reprint, Tuscaloosa: University of Alabama, 2000.

Pate, James P. , ed. *Reminiscences of George Strother Gaines: A Pioneer and Statesman of Early Alabama and Mississippi, 1805–1843*. Tuscaloosa: University of Alabama Press, 1998.

Peake, Ora B. *A History of the United States Indian Factory System, 1795–1822*. Denver: Sage Books, 1954.

Pickett, Albert J. *History of Alabama, and Incidentally of Georgia and Mississippi, from the Earliest Period*. 2 vols. Reprint, Spartanburg, S. C.: Reprint Co., 1975.

Pope, John A. *A Tour through the Southern and Western Territories of the United States of North-America*. Reprint, New York: Arno Press, 1975.

Porter, Kenneth W. *The Negro on the American Frontier*. Gainesville: University of Florida Press, 1975.

Potter, Dorothy Williams. *Passports of Southeastern Pioneers 1770–1823*. Baltimore: Gateway Press, 1982.

Proctor, Samuel, ed. *Eighteenth-Century Florida and Its Borderlands*. Gainesville: University of Florida, 1975.

Prucha, Francis P. "American Indian Policy in the 1840s: Visions of Reform." In *The Frontier Challenge: Responses to the Trans-Mississippi West*. John G. Clark, ed. Lawrence: University of Kansas Press, 1971.

———. "Andrew Jackson's Indian Policy: A Reassessment." *Journal of American History* 56 (1969): 527–39.

Quaife, Milo M., ed. *The Preston and Virginia Papers of the Draper Collection of Manuscripts.* Publications of the State Historical Society of Wisconsin, Calendar Series, vol. 1. Madison: The Society, 1915.

Rea, Robert, and Milo B. Howard, Jr. *The Minutes, Journals, and Acts of the General Assembly of British West Florida.* Tuscaloosa, University of Alabama Press, 1979.

Romans, Bernard. *A Concise Natural History of East and West Florida: Containing an Account of the Natural Produce of All the Southern Part of British America in the Three Kingdoms of Nature, Particularly the Animal and Vegetable.* 1775. Reprint, Tuscaloosa: University of Alabama Press, 1999.

Rowland, Dunbar, ed. *Mississippi Provincial Archives, English Dominion.* Nashville: Brandon Printing Co., 1911.

————, ed., and Albert G. Sanders, translator. *Mississippi Provincial Archives, 1701–1743, French Dominion.* 3 vols. Jackson: Mississippi Department of Archives and History, 1927–32.

———— and Patricia Kay Galloway, eds. *Mississippi Provincial Archives, French Dominion,* vol. 4, *1729–1748;* vol. 5, *1759–63.* Baton Rouge: Louisiana State University Press, ca. 1984.

Satz, Ronald H. *American Indian Policy in the Jacksonian Era.* Lincoln: University of Nebraska Press, 1975.

Saunders, William L., ed., *The Colonial Records of North Carolina.* 10 vols. Raleigh: P. M. Hale, 1896–90.

Schoolcraft, Henry R. *Historical and Statistical Information Respecting the History, Condition, and Prospects of the Indian Tribes of the United States.* 1851. Reprint, New York: Paladin Press, 1969.

Shaw, Helen Louise. *British Administration of the Southern Indians, 1756–1783.* New York: Arno Press, 1981.

Sheehan, Bernard W. *Seeds of Extinction: Jeffersonian Philanthropy and the American Indian.* Chapel Hill: University of North Carolina Press, 1973.

Schmeckebier, Laurence. *The Office of Indian Affairs: Its History, Activities, and Organization.* 1927. Reprint, New York: AMS Press, 1972.

Spencer, Robert F., ed. *The Native Americans: Ethnology and Backgrounds of the North American Indians.* New York: Harper & Row, ca. 1977.

Swanton, John R. *Aboriginal Culture of the Southeast*. Washington: Government Printing Office, 1928.

———. *Indian Tribes of the Lower Mississippi Valley and Adjacent Coast of the Gulf of Mexico*. 1911. Reprint, St. Clair Shores, Mich.: Scholarly Press, 1976.

———. *The Indian Tribes of North America*. 1952. Reprint, Grosse Pointe, Mich.: Scholarly Press, 1968.

———. *The Indians of the Southeastern United States*. Washington: Smithsonian Institution, 1979.

———. *Myths and Tales of the Southeastern Indians*. 1929. Reprint, Norman: University of Oklahoma Press, 1995.

———. *Source Material for the Social and Ceremonial Life of the Choctaw Indians*. Smithsonian Institution, Bureau of American Ethnology, Bulletin 103. Washington: Government Printing Office, 1931.

Usner, Daniel H. Jr. *Indians, Settlers, and Slaves in a Frontier Exchange Economy: The Lower Mississippi Valley before 1783*. Chapel Hill: University of North Carolina Press, 1992.

Waldman, Carl. *Atlas of the North American Indian*. New York: Facts on File, 1985.

Way, Royal B. "The United States Factory System for Trading with the Indians, 1796–1822." *Mississippi Valley Historical Review* 6 (1919–20): 220–35.

Weber, David J. *The Spanish Frontier in North America*. New Haven: Yale University Press, 1992.

Williams, Walter E., ed. *Southeastern Indians since the Removal Era*. Athens: University of Georgia Press, ca. 1979.

Willis, William S. "Divide and Rule: Red, White, and Black in the Southeast." *Journal of Negro History* 48 (1974): 157–76.

Wissler, Clark. *Indians of the United States*. Rev. ed. Lucy Wales Kluckhorn, ed. Garden City, N.Y.: Anchor Books, 1966.

Witcher, Curt B., and George J. Nixon. "Tracking Native American Family History." In *The Source: A Guidebook of American Genealogy*. Loretto Dennis Szucs and Sandra Hargreaves Luebking, eds. Salt Lake City: Ancestry, 1997: 521–72.

Wood, Peter H.; Gregory A. Waselkov; and M. Thomas Hatley, eds. *Powhatan's Mantle: Indians in the Colonial Southeast*. Lincoln: University of Nebraska Press, ca. 1989.

Woods, Patricia Dillon. *French-Indian Relations on the Southern Frontier, 1699–1762.* Ann Arbor: UMI Research Press, 1980.

Wright, J. Leitch Jr. *Britain and the American Frontier 1783–1815.* Athens: University of Georgia Press, 1975.

———. *The Only Land They Knew: The Tragic Story of the American Indians of the Old South.* New York: Free Press, 1981.

Young, Mary E. *Redskins, Ruffleshirts, and Rednecks: Indian Allotments in Alabama and Mississippi, 1830–1860.* Norman: University of Oklahoma Press, 1961.

CHEROKEE

Anderson, Rufus. *Memoir of Catharine Brown, a Christian Indian of the Cherokee Nation.* 1875. Reprint, Tuscaloosa, Ala.: Confederate Publishing Co., 1986.

Anderson, William L., ed. *Cherokee Removal, Before and After.* Athens: University of Georgia Press, 1991.

——— and James A. Lewis. *A Guide to Cherokee Documents in Foreign Archives.* Native American Bibliography Series, no. 4. Metuchen, N. J.: Scarecrow Press, 1983.

Baker, Jack D. *Cherokee Emigration Rolls, 1817–1835.* Oklahoma City: Baker Publishing Co., 1977.

Bartram, William. *Travels through North and South Carolina, Georgia, East and West Florida, the Cherokee Country, the Extensive Territories of the Muscogulges or Creek Confederacy, and the Country of the Choctaws.* 1791. Reprint, Beehive Press, 1973.

Blankenship, Bob. *Cherokee Roots,* vol. 1, *Eastern Cherokee Rolls;* vol. 2, *Western Cherokee Rolls.* Cherokee, N.C.: Privately printed, 1992.

———. *Guion Miller Roll "Plus" of Eastern Cherokee East & West of Mississippi, "1909."* Cherokee, N.C.: Privately printed, ca. 1994.

Brown, John P. *Old Frontiers: The Story of the Cherokee Indians from Earliest Times to the Date of their Removal to the West, 1838.* Kingsport, Tenn.: Southern Publishers, 1938.

Carter, Kent. "Deciding Who Can Be Cherokee: Enrollment Records of the Dawes Commission." *Chronicles of Oklahoma* 69 (1991): 174–205.

——. "Federal Indian Policy: Cherokee Enrollment, 1891–1907." *Prologue* 23 (1991): 25–38.

Cashion, Jerry Clyde. *Fort Butler and the Cherokee Indian Removal from North Carolina*. Raleigh: Privately Printed [?], 1970.

Chase, Marybelle W. *1842 Cherokee Claims, Saline District*. Tulsa: Privately printed, 1988.

——. *1842 Cherokee Claims, Skin Bayou District*. Tulsa: Privately printed, 1988.

——. *1851 Cherokee Old Settlers Annuity Roll*. Tulsa: Privately printed, 1993.

——. *Cherokee Drennen Roll of 1851*. Tulsa: Privately printed, 1994.

——. *Records of the Cherokee Agency in Tennessee, 1801–1835*. Tulsa, Okla.: Privately printed, n.d.

Corkran, David H. *The Cherokee Frontier: Conflict and Survival, 1740–62*. Norman: University of Oklahoma Press, 1962.

Conser, Walter H., Jr. "John Ross and the Cherokee Resistance Campaign, 1833–1838." *Journal of Southern History* 44 (1978): 191–212.

Eaton, Rachel Caroline. *John Ross and the Cherokee Indians*. Menasha, Wisc.: George Banta Publishing Co., 1914.

Ehle, John. *Trail of Tears: The Rise and Fall of the Cherokee Nation*. New York: Doubleday, 1988.

Finger, John R. "The Abortive Second Cherokee Removal, 1841–1844." *Journal of Southern History* 47 (1981): 207–26.

——. *The Eastern Band of Cherokees, 1819–1900*. Knoxville: University of Tennessee Press, 1984.

Fitzgerald, Mary N. *The Cherokee and His Smoky Mountain Legends*. 3rd ed. Asheville, N. C.: Stephens Press, 1946.

——. *The Cherokees*. Knoxville: Clarence F. Coleman Co., 1939.

Foreman, Grant. *Sequoyah*. Norman: University of Oklahoma Press, 1938.

Gilbert, William H., Jr. *The Cherokees of North Carolina: Living Memorials of the Past*. Washington: N.p., 1957.

——. *Eastern Cherokee Social Organization*. Chicago: N.p., 1935.

——. *The Eastern Cherokees*. 1943. Reprint, New York: AMS Press, 1978.

———— and Stephen A. Langone. *The National Significance of the Chero-kee Indians*. Washington: Government Printing Office, 1962.

Gilliam, Frankie Sue. *Cherokee Ancestry Resource Guide*. Muskogee: Twin Territories Publishing Co., 2000.

Gormley, Myra Vanderpool. *Cherokee Connections: An Introduction to Genealogical Sources Pertaining to Cherokee Ancestors*. Baltimore: Genealogical Publishing Co., 1998.

Halliburton, R., Jr. "Black Slave Control in the Cherokee Nation." *The Journal of Ethnic Studies* 3 (1975): 23–35.

————. "Origins of Black Slavery among the Cherokees." *Chronicles of Oklahoma* 52 (1974–5): 483–96.

Harmon, George D. "The North Carolina Cherokees and the New Echota Treaty of 1835." *North Carolina Historical Review* 6 (1929): 237–53.

Hatley, Tom. *The Dividing Paths: Cherokees and South Carolinians through the Era of Revolution*. New York: Oxford University Press, 1993.

Hoig, Stan. *Sequoyah:The Cherokee Genius*. Oklahoma City: Oklahoma Historical Society, 1995.

————. "The Catawba Indians of South Carolina: A Question of Ethnic Survival." In *Southeastern Indians since the Removal Era*, Walter L. Williams, ed. Athens, University of Georgia Press, ca. 1979. Pages 110–20.

Jordan, Jerry Wright. *Cherokee by Blood: Records of Eastern Cherokee Ancestry in the U. S. Court of Claims, 1906–1910*. 9 vols. Bowie, Md.: Heritage Books, 1987–97.

Kutsche, Paul. *A Guide to Cherokee Documents in the Northeastern United States*. Native American Bibliography Series, no. 7. Metuchen, N. J.: Scarecrow Press, 1986.

————. "The Tsali Legend: Culture Heroes and Historiography." *Ethnohistory* 10 (1963): 329–57.

McClure, Tony Mack. *Cherokee Proud: A Guide for Tracing and Honoring Your Cherokee Ancestors*. Somerville, Tenn.: Chunannee Books, 1999.

McLoughlin, William G. *Champions of the Cherokees: Evan and John B. Jones*. Princeton: Princeton University Press, 1990.

————. *Cherokees and Missionaries, 1789–1839*. New Haven: Yale University Press, 1984.

————. "Thomas Jefferson and the Beginning of Cherokee Nationalism, 1806 to 1809." *William and Mary Quarterly*. 3d series 32 (1975): 547–80.

Mails, Thomas E. *The Cherokee People: The Story of the Cherokees From Earliest Origins to Contemporary Times*. New York: Marlowe, 1994.

McKee, John, Papers of. MSS, ca. 1792–1825, Library of Congress. 875 items heavily dealing with Cherokee, Chickasaw, and Choctaw nations, among whom McKee served as U. S. agent.

Mooney, Thomas G. *Exploring Your Cherokee Ancestors: A Basic Genealogical Research Guide*. Tahlequah: Cherokee National Historical Society, 1990.

Moulton, Gary E., ed. *The Papers of Chief John Ross*. Norman: University of Oklahoma Press, 1985.

O'Donnell, James, III. *The Cherokees of North Carolina in the American Revolution*. Knoxville: University of Tennessee Press, 1973.

Parins, James W. *John Rollin Ridge: His Life & Works*. Lincoln: University of Nebraska Press, ca. 1991.

Perdue, Theda. *Slavery and the Evolution of Cherokee Society, 1540–1866*. Knoxville: University of Tennessee Press, 1979.

————. *Cherokee Women: Gender and Culture Change, 1700–1835*. Lincoln: University of Nebraska Press, 1998.

Phillips, Joyce B. and Paul Gary Phillips, eds. *The Brainerd Journal: A Mission to the Cherokees, 1817–1823*. Lincoln: University of Nebraska Press, ca. 1998.

Rights, Douglas L. *The American Indian in North Carolina*. Winston-Salem. N.C.: J. F. Blair, 1957.

Rozema, Vicki. *Footsteps of the Cherokees: A Guide to the Eastern Homelands of the Cherokee Nation*. Winston-Salem, N.C.: J. F. Blair, 1995.

Satz, Ronald N. *Tennessee's Indian Peoples: From White Contact to Indian Removal, 1540–1840*. Knoxville: University of Tennessee Press, 1979.

Serrano y Sanz, Manuel. *España y los indios Cherokis y Chactas en la segunda mitad del siglo xviii*. Seville: Tip. de la "Guía official," 1916.

Serrano y Sanz, Manuel. *Spain and the Cherokee and Choctaw Indians in the Second Half of the Eighteenth Century*, translated by Samuel D. Dickinson. Idabel, Okla.: Privately printed[?], 1995.

Shadburn, Don L. *Cherokee Planters in Georgia, 1832–1838: Historical Essays on Eleven Counties in the Cherokee Nation of Georgia*. Roswell, Ga.: W. H. Wolfe Associates, 1989.

Siler, David W. *The Eastern Cherokee: A Census of the Cherokee Nation in North Carolina, Tennessee, Alabama, and Georgia in 1851*. Cottonport, La.: Polyanthos, 1972.

Strickland, Rennard. *Fire and the Spirits: Cherokee Law from Clan to Courts*. Norman: University of Oklahoma Press, 1975.

Stringfield, William W. "North Carolina Cherokee Indians." *The North Carolina Booklet* 3 (1903): 5–24.

Stuart, John. *A Sketch of the Cherokee and Choctaw Indians*. Little Rock: Woodruff and Pew, 1837.

Wilkins, Thurman. *Cherokee Tragedy: The Ridge Family and the Decimation of a People*. 2nd ed. Norman: University of Oklahoma Press, 1986.

Williams, David. *The Georgia Gold Rush: Twenty-Niners, Cherokees, and Gold Fever*. Columbia: University of South Carolina Press, 1993.

Wilms, Douglas C. "Cherokee Settlement Patterns in Nineteenth- Century Georgia. " *Southeastern Geographer* 14 (1974): 46–53.

Woodward, Grace Steele. *The Cherokees*. Civilization of American Indian series, vol. 65. Norman: University of Oklahoma Press, 1963.

CHICKASAW

Alexander Moore, ed. *Nairne's Muskhogean Journals: The 1708 Expedition to the Mississippi River*. Jackson: University Press of Mississippi, 1988.

Atkinson, James R. *History of the Chickasaw Indian Agency East of the Mississippi River*. Starkville, Miss.: Privately printed, 1998.

Baird, W. David. *The Chickasaw People*. Phoenix: Indian Tribal Series, 1974.

Chickasaws and Choctaws: A Pamphlet of Information Concerning Their History, Treaties, Government, Country, Laws, Politics, and Affairs. Wilmington, Del.: Scholarly Resources, 1975.

Cushman, Horatio Bardwell. *History of the Choctaw, Chickasaw and Natchez Indians*. Greenville, Texas: Headlight Printing House, 1899.

Doherty, Craig A. and Katherine M. *The Chickasaw*. Vero Beach, Fla.: Rourke Publications, 1994.

The Expedition of Baron de Longueuil. Harrisburg: Pennsylvania Historical Commission, 1940.

Gibson, Arrell M. *The Chickasaws*. Norman: University of Oklahoma Press, 1971.

Hale, Duane K.; Arrell M. Gibson; and Frank W. Porter III. *The Chickasaw*. New York: Chelsea House Publishers, ca. 1991.

Hall, James. *A Brief History of the Mississippi Territory, to Which is Prefixed a Summary View of the Country between the Settlements on Cumberland River & the Territory*. Spartanburg, S.C.: Reprint Co., 1976.

Harris, John Brice. *From Old Mobile to Fort Assumption; a Story of the French Attempts to Colonize Louisiana, and Destroy the Chickasaw Indians*. Nashville: Parthenon Press, 1959.

Hoyt, Anne Kelley. *Bibliography of the Chickasaw*. Metuchen, N.J.: Scarecrow Press, 1987.

Lankford, George E. and W. K. McNeil. *Native American Legends: Southeastern Legends—Tales from the Natchez, Caddo, Biloxi, Chickasaw, and Other Nations*. American Folklore Series. Little Rock: August House, 1987.

Littlefield, Daniel F., Jr. *The Chickasaw Freedmen: A People Without a Country*. Westport, Conn.: Greenwood Press, 1980.

Malone, James H. *The Chickasaw Nation*. Louisville, Ky.: J. P. Morton & Co., 1927.

McKee, John, Papers of. MSS, ca. 1792–1825, Library of Congress. 875 items heavily dealing with Cherokee, Chickasaw, and Choctaw nations, among whom McKee served as U. S. agent.

Mosley, John W., ed. *A Record of Missionary Meetings Held in the Chahta and Chikesha Nations and the Records of Tombigbee Presbytery from 1825 to 1838*. West Point, Miss.: West Point Leader, n.d.

Riggs Family Papers, 1763–1945. MSS. Library of Congress, Washington, D.C.: 100,000 items, 3 rolls microfilm. Includes papers relating to 1843 settlement of Chickasaw and Choctaw Land Claims.

Snyder, Clifford Gene, ed. *In the Land of the Chickasaw: Early Travels, Observations, and Historical Descriptions*. North Hollywood, Calif: Jesco, 1997.

Sumners, Cecil L. *Chief Tishomingo: A History of the Chickasaw Indians, and Some Historical Events of their Era (1737–1839)*. Iuka, Miss., Sumners, 1974.

———. *The Trial of Chief Tishomingo: The Last Great War Chief of the Chickasaw Indians*. Iuka, Miss.: Sumners, 1977.

Swanton, John R. *Social and Religious Beliefs and Usages of the Chickasaw Indians*. Washington: Government Printing Office, 1928.

Williams, Samuel Cole. *Beginnings of West Tennessee, in the Land of the Chickasaws, 1541–1841*. Johnson City, Tenn.: Watauga Press, 1930.

Wiltshire, Betty C., comp. *Choctaw and Chickasaw Early Census Records*. Carrollton, Miss.: Pioneer Publishing Co., ca.1997.

CHOCTAW

Baird, W. David. *Peter Pitchlynn: Chief of the Choctaw*. Norman: University of Oklahoma Press, 1986.

Bartram, William. *Travels through North and South Carolina, Georgia, East and West Florida, the Cherokee Country, the Extensive Territories of the Muscogulges or Creek Confederacy, and the Country of the Choctaws*. 1791. Reprint, Beehive Press, 1973.

Bekkers, M. J. "History of the Indian Mission of Tucker, Neshoba County, Mississippi." Typescript copy of the journal of Fr. Bekkers. Holy Rosary Mission, Tucker, Miss., n.d.

Blanchard, Kendall. *The Mississippi Choctaw at Play: The Serious Side of Leisure*. Urbana: University of Illinois Press, 1981.

Bremer, Cora. *The Chata Indians of Pearl River*. New Orleans: Picayune Job Print, ca.1907.

Bushnell, David I., Jr. *The Choctaw of Bayou Lacomb, St. Tammany Parish, Louisiana*. Smithsonian Institution, Bureau of American Ethnology Bulletin 48. Washington: Government Printing Office, 1909.

———. *Myths of the Louisiana Choctaw*. Lancaster, Pa.: New Era Printing Co., 1911.

Byington, Cyrus. *A Dictionary of the Choctaw Language*. John R. Swanton and Henry S. Halbert, eds. Washington: Government Printing Office, 1915.

Carson, James Taylor. *Searching for the Bright Path: The Mississippi Choctaws from Prehistory to Removal*. Lincoln: University of Nebraska Press, ca. 1999.

Carter, Kent. *Records of the Bureau of Indian Affairs: Records of the Five Civilized Tribes; Agency Records Relating to the Identification of Mississippi Choctaws, 1899–1904*. Microcopy 7RA116, 2 rolls. Fort Worth: National Archives—Southwest Region, n.d.

Chickasaws and Choctaws: A Pamphlet of Information Concerning Their History, Treaties, Government, Country, Laws, Politics, and Affairs. Wilmington, Del.: Scholarly Resources, 1975.

Cushman, Horatio Bardwell. *History of the Choctaw, Chickasaw, and Natchez Indians*. Greenville, Texas: Headlight Printing House, 1899.

Debo, Angie. *The Rise and Fall of the Choctaw Republic*. Norman: University of Oklahoma Press, 1934.

Galloway, Patricia. *Choctaw Genesis, 1500–1700*. Lincoln: University of Nebraska Press, ca. 1995.

Goss, Joe R., ed. *A Complete Roll of All Choctaw Claimants and Their Heirs*. Conway, Ark.: Oldbuck Press, ca. 1992. (An index to the published claim abstracts itemized below under U. S. Court of Claims.)

———, ed. *The Choctaw Academy: Official Correspondence, 1825–1941*. Conway, Ark.: Oldbuck Press, n.d.

Halbert, Henry Sale. "Choctaw Indian Names in Alabama and Mississippi." *Transactions of the Alabama Historical Quarterly* 3 (1898–99).

———. "District Divisions of the Choctaw Nation." *Publications of the Alabama Historical Quarterly, Misc. Collections* 1 (1901): 375–85.

Hiemstra, William L. "Early Presbyterian Missions among the Choctaw and Chickasaw." *Journal of Mississippi History* 10 (1948): 8–16.

Holmes, Jack D. "The Choctaws in 1795." *Alabama Historical Quarterly* 30 (1968): 33–49.

Kidwell, Clara Sue. *Choctaws and Missionaries in Mississippi, 1818–1918*. Norman: University of Oklahoma Press, 1995.

Lewis, Anna. *Chief Pushmataha, American Patriot: The Story of the Choctaws' Struggle For Survival.* New York: Exposition Press, 1959.

Lusser, J. "Journal of the Journey That I Made in the Choctaw Nation by Order of Mr. Perier, Beginning on January 12th, 1730, and Lasting until March 23rd of the Same Year. " *Mississippi Provincial Archives, French Dominion.* Dunbar Rowland, ed., and A. G. Sanders, transl., 3 vols. Jackson: Mississippi Department of Archives and History, 1927–32. Vol. 1: 81–117.

McBride, Ralph Folsom and Alberta Patrick McBride. *A Family Makes Its Mark: The Leflores of Mississippi.* Jacksonville, Fla.: McBride, 1976.

McKee, John, Papers of. MSS, ca. 1792–1825, Library of Congress, Washington, D.C.. 875 items, primarily dealing with Cherokee, Chickasaw, and Choctaw nations, among whom McKee served as U. S. agent.

Matte, Jacqueline A. *They Say the Wind Is Red: The Alabama Choctaw; Lost in Their Own Land.* Red Level, Ala.: Greenberry Publishing Co., ca. 1999.

Mosley, John W., ed. *A Record of Missionary Meetings Held in the Chahta and Chikesha Nations and the Records of Tombigbee Presbytery from 1825 to 1838.* West Point, Miss.: West Point Leader Printing, n.d.

O'Brien, Greg. "The Conqueror Meets the Unconquered: Negotiating Cultural Boundaries on the Post-Revolutionary Southern Frontier." *Journal of Southern History* 67 (2001): 39–72.

O'Brien, Warren Gregory. "Choctaws in a Revolutionary Age: A Study of Power and Authority, 1750–1801." Ph.D diss., University of Kentucky, 1998.

————. "Protecting Trade through War: Choctaw Elites and British Occupation of the Floridas." In Martin Daunton and Rick Halpern, eds. *Empire and Others: British Encounters with Indigenous Peoples, 1600–1850.* Philadelphia: University of Pennsylvania Press, 1999.

Plaisance, A. "The Choctaw Trading House, 1803–1822." *Alabama Historical Quarterly* 16 (1954): 393–423.

Peterson, John H., Jr. *A Choctaw Source Book.* New York and London: Garland Publishing, 1985.

Ray, Florence Rebecca. *Chieftain Greenwood Leflore and the Choctaw Indians of the Mississippi Valley: Last Chief of Choctaws East of Mississippi River*. 2d ed. Memphis, Tenn.: C. A. David Printing Co., 1936.

Reeves, Carolyn Keller, ed. *The Choctaw before Removal*. Jackson: University Press of Mississippi, 1985.

Riggs Family Papers, 1763–1945. MSS. Library of Congress, Washington, D.C.: 100,000 items, 3 rolls microfilm. Includes papers relating to 1843 settlement of Chickasaw and Choctaw Land Claims.

Sawyer, Charles H. "The Choctaw Indians of Mississippi." *Twin Territories* 4 (1902): 160–64 and 205–11.

Serrano y Sanz, Manuel. *España y los indios Cherokis y Chactas en la segunda mitad del siglo xviii*. Seville: Tip. de la "Guía official," 1916.

———. *Spain and the Cherokee and Choctaw Indians in the Second Half of the Eighteenth Century*, translated by Samuel D. Dickinson. Idabel, Okla.: Privately printed[?], 1995.

Strickland, Ben, Jean Strickland, and P. N. Edwards, comps. *Records of Choctaw Trading Post, St. Stephens, Mississippi Territory*. 2 vols. Moss Point, Miss.: B. & J. Strickland, ca. 1984, 1990.

Stuart, John. *A Sketch of the Cherokee and Choctaw Indians*. Little Rock: Woodruff and Pew, 1837.

Swanton, John. "An Early Account of the Choctaw Indians." *Memoirs of the American Anthropological Association* 5 (1918): 1–118.

———. *Source Material for the Social and Ceremonial Life of the Choctaw Indians*. 1931. Reprint, Tuscaloosa: University of Alabama Press, 2001.

U. S. Court of Claims. *The Choctaw Nation of Indians v. The United States, Case No. 12742: Argument for Claimant*. Washington: R. O. Polkinhorn, ca. 1882. (408 pp. This is a companion volume to the more genealogically valuable publication, *Evidence for Claimant*, immediately below.)

———. *The Choctaw Nation of Indians v. The United States, Case No. 12742: Evidence for Claimant*. Washington: R. O. Polkinhorn[?], ca. 1882, 1898. (880 pp. For an index, see Goss, *A Complete Roll of All Choctaw Claimants*, above.)

Watkins, John A. "A Contribution to Chacta History." *American Antiquarian (and Oriental Journal)* 16 (1894): 257–65.

"William Ward's Register." *Mississippi Genealogical Exchange* 18 (Spring 1972): 11–14.

Wiltshire, Betty C., comp. *Choctaw and Chickasaw Early Census Records*. Carrollton, Miss.: Pioneer Publishing Co., ca. 1997.

Wright, Alfred. "Choctaws, Religious Opinions, Traditions, etc." *Missionary Herald* 24 (1828): 214–16.

24th Cong., 1st sess., H. Doc. 119. *Choctaw Indians*. By Andrew Hays, Agent. February 1, 1836.

27th Cong., 2nd sess., H. Doc. 231. *Choctaw Academy*. May 20, 1842.

CREEK

Bartram, John. "Diary of a Journey through the Carolinas, Georgia, and Florida from July 1, 1765, to April 10, 1766." In Francis Harper, ed. *Transactions of the American Philosophical Society*. New Series 33 (1942). Part 1: 1–120.

Bartram, William. "Observations on the Creek and Cherokee Indians." *Transactions of the American Ethnological Society* 3 (1853), part 1: 1–81.

———. "Travels in Georgia and Florida, 1773–4: A Report to Doctor John Fothergill." *Transactions of the American Philosophical Society*. New series 33 (1943), part 2: 121–242.

———. *Travels through North and South Carolina, Georgia, East and West Florida, the Cherokee Country, the Extensive Territories of the Muscogulges or Creek Confederacy, and the Country of the Choctaws*. 1791. Reprint, Beehive Press, 1973..

Bast, Homer. "Creek Indian Affairs, 1775–1778." *Georgia Historical Quarterly* 33 (1949): 1–25.

Boyd, Mark F. "Horatio S. Dexter and Events Leading to the Treaty of Moultrie Creek with the Seminoles." *Florida Anthropologist* 11 (1958): 65–95.

Bonner, James C. "Tustunugee Hutkee and Creek Factionalism on the Georgia-Alabama Frontier." *Alabama Review* 19 (1957): 111–25.

———. "William McIntosh." In *Georgians in Profile; Historical Essays in Honor of Ellis Merton Coulter*. Athens: University of Georgia Press, 1958. Pages 114–43.

———, ed. "Journal of a Mission to Georgia in 1827." *Georgia Historical Quarterly* 44 (1960): 74–85.

Brannon, Peter A. "Aboriginal Towns in Alabama." *Handbook of the Alabama Anthropological Society*. Montgomery: Brown Printing Co., 1920.

———. "Journal of James A. Tait for the Year 1813." *Georgia Historical Quarterly* 8 (1924): 229–39.

———. *The Southern Indian Trade: Being Particularly a Study of Material from the Tallapoosa River Valley of Alabama*. Montgomery: Paragon Press, 1935.

Braund, Kathryn E. Holland. *Deerskins & Duffels: The Creek Indian Trade with Anglo-America, 1685–1815*. Lincoln, University of Nebraska Press, 1993.

Campbell, Thomas. "Thomas Campbell to Lord Deane Gordon: An Account of the Creek Nation, 1764." *Florida Historical Quarterly* 8 (1930): 156–64.

Carter, Kent. "Snakes and Scribes: The Dawes Commission and the Enrollment of the Creeks." *Prologue* 29 (1997): 28–41.

Cashin, Edward J. *Lachlan McGillivray, Indian Trader: The Shaping of the Southern Colonial Frontier*. Athens: University of Georgia Press, 1992.

Caughey, John W. *McGillivray of the Creeks*. Norman: University of Oklahoma Press, 1938.

Chambers, Nella J. "The Creek Indian Factory at Fort Mitchell." *Alabama Historical Quarterly* 16 (1959): 15–53.

Chapman, George. *Chief William McIntosh: A Man of Two Worlds*. Atlanta: Cherokee Publishing Co., 1988.

Clay, Clement, Mrs. "Recollections of Opothleyoholo." *Arrow Review* 4 (1922): 35–36.

Coley, C. J. "Creek Treaties 1790–1832." *Alabama Review* 11 (1958): 163–76.

Corkran, David H. *The Creek Frontier, 1540–1783*. Norman: University of Oklahoma Press, 1967.

Corry, John Pitts. *Indian Affairs in Georgia, 1732–1756*. New York: AMS Press, 1980.

Coulter, E. Merton. "Mary Musgrove, 'Queen of the Creeks': A Chapter of Early Georgia Troubles." *Georgia Historical Quarterly* 11 (1927): 1–30.

Debo, Angie. *The Road to Disappearance*. Norman: University of Oklahoma Press, 1941.

Doster, James F., ed. "Letters Relating to the Tragedy of Fort Mims," *Alabama Review* 14 (1961): 269–85.

———. *The Creek Indians and Their Florida Lands, 1740–1823*. New York: Garland Publishing, 1974.

Downes, Randolph C. "Creek-American Relations 1782–1790." *Georgia Historical Quarterly* 21 (1937): 142–84.

———. "Creek-American Relations, 1790–1795." *Journal of Southern History* 8 (1942): 350–73.

Downs, Dorothy. "British Influences on Creek and Seminole Men's Clothing, 1733–1858." *Florida Anthropologist* 33 (1980): 46–65.

Edmunds, R. David. *Tecumseh and the Quest for Indian Leadership*. Boston: Little, Brown, and Co., 1984.

Eggleston, George Cary. *Red Eagle and the Wars with the Creek Indians of Alabama*. Reprint, New York: AMS Press, 1980.

Floyd, John. "Letters of John Floyd, 1813–1838." *Georgia Historical Quarterly* 33 (1949): 228–69.

Foreman, Carolyn Thomas. "The White Lieutenant and Some of His Contemporaries." *Chronicles of Oklahoma* 38 (1960): 425–40.

Gatschet, Albert S. *A Migration Legend of the Creek Indians with a Linguistic, Historic, and Ethnographic Introduction*. 1884. Reprint, New York: AMS Press, 1969.

———. *Towns and Villages of the Creek Confederacy in the XVIII and XIX Centuries*. Montgomery, Ala.: Brown Printing Co., 1901.

Goff, John H. "The Path to Oakfuskee, Upper Creek Route in Georgia to the Creek Indians." *Georgia Historical Quarterly* 39 (1955): 1–36.

Grant, C. L., ed. *Letters, Journals and Writings of Benjamin Hawkins*. 2 vols. Savannah: Beehive Press, 1980.

Green, Michael D. "Alexander McGillivray." In *American Indian Leaders: Studies in Diversity*. R. David Edmunds, ed. Lincoln: University of Nebraska Press, 1980.

Griffith, Benjamin W. Jr. "Lt. David Moniac, Creek Indian: First Minority Graduate of West Point." *Alabama Historical Quarterly* 43 (1980): 99–110.

———. *McIntosh and Weatherford, Creek Indian Leaders*. 1980. Reprint, Tuscaloosa: University of Alabama Press, 1998.

Hall, Arthur H. "The Red Stick War: Creek Indian Affairs during the War of 1812." *Chronicles of Oklahoma* 12 (1934): 264–93.

Halbert, Henry S. and T. H. Ball. *The Creek War of 1813 and 1814*. 1895; Reprint. Frank L. Owsley Jr., ed. Tuscaloosa: University of Alabama Press, 1969.

Hawkins, Benjamin. *A Sketch of the Creek Country in the Years 1798 and 1799*. 1848. Reprint, Spartanburg: Reprint Co., 1974.

———. *Letters, Journals, and Writings of Benjamin Hawkins*. 2 vols. C. L. Grant, ed., Savannah: Beehive Press, 1980.

———. *Letters of Benjamin Hawkins, 1796–1806*. Savannah: Georgia Historical Society, 1916.

———. Papers of. MSS. Library of Congress, Washington, D.C. 2 vols., 3 loose items, 1 roll microfilm.

Hays, Louise Frederick, ed. *A Combination of A Sketch of the Creek Country, in the Years 1798 and 1799, and Letters of Benjamin Hawkins, 1796–1806*. Spartanburg, S. C.: Reprint Co., 1974.

Henri, Florette. *The Southern Indians and Benjamin Hawkins, 1796–1816*. Norman: University of Oklahoma Press, 1986.

Holland, James W. "Andrew Jackson and the Creek War: Victory at the Horseshoe." *Alabama Review* 21 (1968): 243–75.

Hook, Jonathan B. *The Alabama-Coushatta Indians*. College Station: Texas A&M University, 1997.

Innerarity, John. "The Creek Nation, Debtor to John Forbes and Company, Successors to Panton, Leslie and Company: A Journal of John Innerarity." *Florida Historical Quarterly* 9 (1930): 67–89.

Kinnaird, Lawrence. "International Rivalry in Creek Country, Part 1: The Ascendancy of Alexander McGillivray, 1783–89." *Florida Historical Quarterly* 10 (1931): 59–85.

Lackey, Richard D. *Frontier Claims in the Lower South: Records of Claims Filed by Citizens of the Alabama and Tombigbee River Settlements in the Mississippi Territory for Depredations by the Creek Indians during the War of 1812*. New Orleans: Polyanthos, 1977.

Letter from the Secretary of the Treasury . . . Relative to the Execution of An Act for the Relief of Samuel Menac, Passed 17th of April 1816. Washington: Gales and Seaton, 1828.

"List of Debts Due by the Traders & Factors of the Upper Creek Towns to the Firm of Messrs. Panton, Leslie & Co. and John Forbes & Co. of Pensacola, adjusted to 1st November 1812." *Florida Historical Quarterly* 9 (1930): 86.

Littlefield, Daniel. *Africans and Creeks*. Westport, Conn.: Greenwood Press, 1979.

Martin, Joel. *Sacred Revolt: The Muskogees' Struggle for a New World*. Boston: Beacon Press, 1991.

Mauelshagen, Carl and Gerald H. David, ed. and trans. *Partners in the Lord's Work: The Diary of Two Moravian Missionaries in the Creek Indian Country, 1807–1813*. Atlanta: Georgia State College, 1969.

Milfort, Louis LeClerc. *Memoir; or, A Cursory Glance at My Different Travels and Sojourn in the Creek Nation*. Ben C. McCary, transl. and ed. Savannah: Beehive Press, 1959.

Meserve, John Bartlett. "Chief Opothleyahola." *Chronicles of Oklahoma* 9 (1932): 439–53.

———. "The Perrymans." *Chronicles of Oklahoma* 15 (1937): 166–84.

Murdock, Richard K., ed. "Mission to the Creek Nation in 1794." *Florida Historical Quarterly* 34 (1955): 266–84.

Neeley, Mary Ann Oglesby. "Lachlan McGillivray: A Scot on the Alabama Frontier." *Alabama Historical Quarterly* 36 (1974): 5–14.

Neill, Wilfred T. "The Galphin Trading Post Site at Silver Bluff, South Carolina." *Florida Anthropologist* 21 (1968): 42–54.

Nunez, Theron A., Jr. "Creek Natavism and the Creek War of 1813–1814." *Ethnohistory* 5 (1958–59): 1–47, 131–75, 292–301.

O'Donnell, James H. "Alexander McGillivray, Training for Leadership." *Georgia Historical Quarterly* 49 (1965): 172–86.

Orrmont, Arthur, *Diplomat in Warpaint: Chief Alexander McGillivrary of the Creeks*. New York: Abelard-Shuman, 1968.

Owsley, Frank L., Jr. "Benjamin Hawkins: The First Modern Indian Agent." *Alabama Historical Quarterly* 30 (1968): 7–13.

_____. "The Fort Mims Massacre." *Alabama Review* 24 (1971): 192–204.

Pickett, Albert J. *History of Alabama and Incidentally of Georgia and Mississippi, from the Earliest Period*. Sheffield, Ala.: R. C. Randolph, 1896.

Pound, Merritt B. "Benjamin Hawkins." In *Georgians in Profile: Historical Essays in Honor of Ellis Merton Coulter*. Athens: University of Georgia Press, 1958. Pages 89–113.

Ross, Daniel J. and Bruce S. Chappell, eds. "Visit to the Indian Nations: The Diary of John Hambly." *Florida Historical Quarterly* 55 (1977): 60–73.

Sattler, Richard A. "Women's Status among the Muscogee and Cherokee." In *Women and Power in Native North America*. Laura F. Klein and Lillian A. Ackermann, eds. Norman: University of Oklahoma Press, 1995.

Sears, William H. "Creek and Cherokee Culture in the Eighteenth Century." *American Antiquity* 21 (1956): 143–49.

Smith, Daniel M. "James Seagrove and the Mission to Tuckaubatchee, 1793." *Georgia Historical Quarterly* 44 (1960): 41–55.

Smoot, Joseph G., ed. "An Account of Alabama Indian Missions and Presbyterian Churches in 1828 from the Travel Diary of William S. Potts." *Alabama Review* 18 (1965): 134–52.

Southerland, Henry D. Jr. and Jerry Elijah Brown. *The Federal Road through Georgia, the Creek Nation, and Alabama: 1806–1836*. Tuscaloosa: University of Alabama Press, 1989.

Spoehr, Alexander. "Changing Kinship Systems: A Study in the Acculturation of the Creeks, Cherokee, and Choctaw." *Field Museum of Natural History Anthropological Series* 33 (1947): 153–235.

Stern, Theodore D. "The Creeks." *The Native Americans: Ethnology and Backgrounds of the North American Indians*. Robert F. Spencer, ed. New York: Harper & Row, ca. 1977. Pages 424–44.

Stiggins, George. *Creek Indian History: A Historical Narrative of the Genealogy, Traditions and Downfall of the Ispocoga or Creek Indian Tribe of Indians, by One of the Tribe*. Virginia P. Brown, ed. 1989. Reprint, Tuscaloosa: University of Alabama Press, 2001.

Sturtevant, William C., ed. *A Creek Source Book*. New York: Garland Publishing, 1987.

———. "Creek into Seminole." In *North American Indians in Historical Perspective*. Eleanor Leacock and Nancy O. Lurie, eds. New York: Random House, 1971. Pages 92–128.

Sugden, John. *Tecumseh: A Life*. New York: Henry Holt, 1997.

Swan, Caleb. "Position and State of Manners and Arts in the Creek, or Muscogee Nation in 1791." In Henry R. Schoolcraft, *North American Indians in Historical Perspective*. 6 vols., 1851–57. Reprint, New York: Paladin Press, 1969. Vol. 5:251–83.

Swanton, John R. *Early History of the Creek Indians and Their Neighbors*. Smithsonian Institution, Bureau of American Ethnology Bulletin 73. Washington: Government Printing Office: 1922.

———. *Religious Beliefs and Medicinal Practices of the Creek Indians*. Washington: Government Printing Office, 1928.

———. *Social Organization and Social Usages of the Indians of the Creek Confederacy*. Washington: Bureau of American Ethnology, 1928.

Taitt, David. "Journal of David Taitt's Travels from Pensacola, West Florida to and through the Country of the Upper and Lower Creeks, 1772." In *Travels in the American Colonies*, Newton D. Mereness, ed. New York: Macmillan Co., 1916.

Tarvin, Marion Elisha. "The Muscoges or Creek Indians from 1517–1893." *Baldwin County Historical Society Quarterly* 8 (1980): 8–21.

Twiggs, John, Gen. "The Creek Troubles of 1793." *Georgia Historical Quarterly* 11 (1927): 274–80.

Watson, Thomas D. "Striving for Sovereignty: Alexander McGillivray, Creek Warfare, and Diplomacy, 1783–1790." *Florida Historical Quarterly* 58 (1980): 400–14.

West, Elizabeth Howard. "A Prelude to the Creek War of 1813–1814 in a Letter of John Innerarity to James Innerarity." *Florida Historical Quarterly* 18 (1940): 247–66.

Young, Mary E. *Redskins, Ruffleshirts, and Rednecks: Indian Allotments in Alabama and Mississippi*. Norman: University of Oklahoma Press, 1961.

Woodward, Thomas S. *The American Old West: Woodward's Reminiscences; A Personal Account of the Creek Nation in Georgia and Alabama*. Mobile: Southern University Press. 1965.

―――. *Woodward's Reminiscences of the Creek, or Muscogee Indians, Contained in Letters to Friends in Georgia and Alabama*. Montgomery, Ala.: Berrett & Wimbish, 1859.

Wright, J. Lietch, Jr. *Creeks and Seminoles*. Lincoln: University of Nebraska Press, 1986.

SEMINOLE

Adams, George R. "Caloosahatchee Massacre: Its Significance in the Second Seminole War." *Florida Historical Quarterly* 48 (1970): 368–80.

Bittle, George C. "The First Battle of the Second Seminole War." *Florida Historical Quarterly* 46 (1967): 39–45.

Blassingame, Wyatt. *Seminoles of Florida*. Tallahassee: Florida Department of Agriculture, 1959.

Boyd, Mark F. "Horatio S. Dexter and Events Leading to the Treaty of Moultrie Creek with the Seminoles." *Florida Anthropologist* 11 (1958): 65–95.

―――. Hale G. Smith, and John W. Griffin, eds. *Here They Once Stood*. Gainesville: University of Florida Press, 1999.

Buker, George E. "Francis's Metallic Life Boats and the Third Seminole War." *Florida Historical Quarterly* 58 (1984): 139–51.

Chamberlain, Donald L. "Fort Brooke: Frontier Outpost, 1824–1842." *Tampa Bay History* 7 (1985): 5–29.

Coe, Charles H. *Red Patriots: The Story of the Seminoles*. 1898. Reprint, Gainesville: University Presses of Florida, 1974.

Covington, James W. *The Billy Bowlegs War, 1855–1858: The Final Stand of the Seminoles against the Whites*. Clulota, Fla.: Mickler House Publishers, 1982.

―――. *The Seminoles of Florida*. Gainesville: University of Florida, 1993.

―――. "Migration of the Seminoles into Florida, 1700–1820." *Florida Historical Quarterly* 46 (1968): 340–57.

―――. "The Agreement of 1842 and Its Effect upon Seminole History." *Florida Anthropologist* 31 (1978): 8–11.

————, ed. *The British Meet the Seminoles*. Contributions of the Florida State Museum: Social Sciences no. 7. Gainesville: University of Florida Press, 1961.

Davis, T. Frederick. "Milly Francis and Duncan McKrimmon, an Authentic Florida Pocahontas." *Florida Historical Quarterly* 21 (1943): 251–58.

Doster, James F. *The Creek Indians and Their Florida Lands, 1740–1823*. 2 vols. New York: Garland Publishers, 1974.

Downs, Dorothy. "British Influences on Creek and Seminole Men's Clothing, 1733–1858." *Florida Anthropologist* 33 (1980): 46–65.

Emerson, William Canfield. *The Seminoles: Dwellers of the Everglades: The Land, History, and Culture of the Florida Indians*. New York: Exposition Press, 1954.

Fairbanks, Charles H. *The Florida Seminole People*. Phoenix: Indian Tribal Series, 1973.

Fairlie, Margaret C. *Stories of the Seminoles*. New York: Rand, McNally & Co., 1928.

Fishburne, Charles C., Jr. *Of Chiefs and Generals: A History of the Cedar Keys to the End of the Second Seminole War*. Cedar Key, Fla.: Sea Hawk Publications, ca. 1982.

Foreman, Carolyn T. "Billy Bowlegs." *Chronicles of Oklahoma* 33 (1955): 512–22.

Forry, Samuel. "Letters of Samuel Forry, Surgeon, U. S. Army, 1837–38." *Florida Historical Quarterly* 6 (1928): 133–48, 206–19; 7 (1928): 88–105.

Garbarino, Merwyn S. *The Seminole*. New York: Chelsea House, 1989.

Giddings, Joshua R. *The Exiles of Florida*. 1858. Reprint, New York: Arno Press, 1969.

Glenn, James Lafayette. *My Work among the Florida Seminoles*. Harry A. Kersey Jr., ed. Orlando: University Presses of Florida, ca. 1982.

Goggin, John M. "Source Materials for the Study of the Florida Seminole Indians." Laboratory Notes no. 3. Gainesville: University of Florida, Anthropology Department, 1959.

Holmes, Jack D. L. "The Southern Boundary Commission, the Chattahoochee River and the Florida Seminoles, 1799." *Florida Historical Quarterly* 44 (1966): 265–84.

Hardlicka, Alex. *The Anthropology of Florida*. Deland: Florida State Historical Society, 1922.

Leo de Belmont, Laura Ana. *Seminole Kinship System and Clan Interaction*. Mendoza, Argentina: Facultad de Filosofía y Letras, Universidad Nacional de Cuyo, 1985.

Littlefield, Daniel F., Jr. *Africans and Seminoles: From Removal to Emancipation*. Westport, Conn.: Greenwood Press, 1977.

Lantz, Raymond C. *Seminole Indians of Florida, 1850–1874*. Bowie, Md.: Heritage Books, 1994.

McCauley, Clay. The *Seminole Indians of Florida*. 1887. Reprint, Gainesville: University Press of Florida, ca. 2000.

McReynolds, Edwin C. *The Seminoles*. Norman: University of Oklahoma Press, 1957.

Mahon, John K. *History of the Second Seminole War, 1835–42*. Gainesville: University of Florida Press, 1967.

————. "Two Seminole Treaties: Paynes' Landing, 1832, and Fort Gibson, 1833." *Florida Historical Quarterly* 41 (1962): 1–21.

Moore-Willson, Minnie. *The Seminoles of Florida*. 1896. Reprint, New York: Moffat, Yard, and Co., 1911.

Motte, Jacob R. *Journey into Wilderness: An Army Surgeon's Account of Life in Camp and Field during the Creek and Seminoles Wars, 1836–1838*. James F. Sunderman, ed. Gainesville: University of Florida Press, 1953.

Mulroy, Kevin. *Freedom on the Border: The Seminole Maroons in Florida, the Indian Territory, Coahuila, and Texas*. Lubbock: Texas Tech University Press, ca. 1993.

Narrative of the Life and Sufferings of Mrs. Jane Johns, Who Was Barbarously Wounded and Scalped by Seminole Indians in East Florida. Baltimore: Jas. Lucas & E. K. Deaver, 1837.

Narrative of the Seminole War and the Miraculous Escape of Mary Godfrey. New York: Garland Publishing, 1977.

Peters, Virginia B. *The Florida Wars*. Hamden, Conn.: Archon Books, 1979.

Porter, Kenneth W. "Billy Bowlegs (Holata Micco) in the Seminole Wars." *Florida Historical Quarterly* 45 (1967): 219–42.

————. "The Founder of the 'Seminole Nation'; Secoffee or Cowkeeper." *Florida Historical Quarterly* 27 (1949): 362–84.

————. "Negroes and the Seminole War, 1835–1842." *Journal of Southern History* 30 (1964): 427–50.

————. "Tholnoto-sassa: A Note on an Obscure Seminole Village in the Early 1820s." *Florida Anthropologist* 13 (1960): 113–19.

————.*The Black Seminoles: History of a Freedom-Seeking People.* Revised ed. Alcione M. Amos and Thomas P. Senter, eds.. Gainesville: University Press of Florida, ca. 1996.

Potter, Woodburne. *The War in Florida: Being an Exposition of Its Causes and an Accurate History of the Campaigns of Generals Clinch, Gaines, and Scott.* Baltimore: Lewis & Coleman, 1836.

Proctor, Samuel, ed. *Eighteenth-Century Florida and Its Borderlands.* Gainesville: University of Florida Press, 1975.

Ramsey, David, ed. "Abner Doubleday and the Third Seminole War." *Florida Historical Quarterly* 59 (1981): 314–34.

Seminole Papers. MSS. Florida Historical Society, University of South Florida, Tampa.

Simmons, William H. *Notices of East Florida with an Account of the Seminole Nation of Indians by a Recent Traveller in the Province.* Charleston: A. E. Miller, 1822.

Sprague, John T. *The Origin, Progress, and Conclusion of the Florida War.* New York: Appleton, 1848.

Sturtevant, William C. *A Seminole Source Book.* New York: Garland Publishers, 1987.

————. "Creek into Seminole." In *North American Indians in Historical Perspective.* Eleanor B. Leacock and Nancy O. Lurie, eds. New York: Random House, 1971.

Swanton, John R. *Creek Religion and Medicine.* 1928. Reprint, Lincoln: University of Nebraska Press, ca. 2000.

————. *Early History of the Creek Indians and Their Neighbors.* 1922. Reprint, Gainesville: University Press of Florida, ca. 1998.

————. *Modern Square Grounds of the Creek Indians.* Washington: Smithsonian Institution, 1931.

The Trials of A. Arbuthnot and R. C. Ambrister, Charged with Inciting the Seminole Indians to War. London: James Ridgeway, 1819.

Webb, Alexander S. "Campaigning in Florida in 1855." *Journal of the Military Service Institutions* (1912): 399–429.

Weisman, Brent R. "On the Trail of Osceola's Seminoles in Florida." Paper distributed by the Order of Indian Wars, January 1988.

———. *Unconquered People: Florida's Seminole and Miccosukee Indians*. Gainesville: University Press of Florida, ca. 1999.

Welch, Andrew. *A Narrative of the Early Days and Remembrances of Osceola Nikkandochee, Prince of Econchati, a Young Seminole Indian, Son of Econchati-Mico, King of the Red Hills in Florida*. 1841. Reprint. Frank Laumer, ed. Gainesville: University of Florida Press, 1977.

Wickman, Patricia R. *Osceola's Legacy*. Tuscaloosa: University of Alabama Press, 1994.

White, Frank E., ed. "Macomb's Mission to the Seminoles: John T. Sprague's Journal Kept during April and May 1839." *Florida Historical Quarterly* 35 (October 1956): 130–93.

Williams, John Lee. *The Territory of Florida*. New York: Goodrich, 1837.

Wright, J. Lietch, Jr. *Creeks and Seminoles*. Lincoln: University of Nebraska Press, 1986.

———. "A Note on the First Seminole War as Seen by the Indians, Negroes, and Their British Advisers." *Journal of Southern History* 34 (1968):565–75.

———. *William Augustus Bowles, Director-General of the Creek Nation*. Athens: University of Georgia Press, 1967.

MISCELLANEOUS TRIBES

Blu, Karen I. *The Lumbee Problem: The Making of American Indian People*. Cambridge, Eng.: Cambridge University Press, 1980.

Bradford, William Rufus. *The Catawba Indians of South Carolina*. Columbia: University Extension Library Service, 1946.

Brown, Douglas Summers. *The Catawba Indians: The People of the River*. Columbia: University of South Carolina Press, 1966.

Bushnell, David I. *The Manahoac Tribes in Virginia, 1608*. Washington: Smithsonian Institution, 1935.

Chamberlain, Alexander Francis. *The Catawba Language*. Toronto: Imrie & Graham, 1888.

Covington, James W. "Proposed Catawba Indian Removal, 1848." *South Carolina Historical and Genealogical Magazine* 55 (1954): 42–47.

Cushman, Horatio Bardwell. *History of the Choctaw, Chickasaw, and Natchez Indians*. Greenville, Texas: Headlight Printing House, 1899.

Dorsey, James Owen and John R. Swanton. *A Dictionary of the Biloxi and Of Languages Accompanied with Thirty-one Biloxi Texts and Numerous Biloxi Phrases*. 1912. Reprint, St. Clair Shores, Mich.: Scholarly Press, 1976.

Feest, Christian F. *The Powhatan Tribes*. New York: Chelsea House Publications, 1990.

Gatschet, Albert Samuel and John R. Swanton. *A Dictionary of the Atakapa Language Accompanied by Text Material*. Washington: Government Printing Office, 1932.

Gilbert, William Harlen. *The Wesorts of Southern Maryland: An Outcast Group*. N.p., 1945.

Gleach, Frederic W. *Powhatan's World and Colonial Virginia: A Conflict of Cultures*. Lincoln: University of Nebraska Press, ca. 1997.

Hudson, Charles M. *The Catawba Nation*. Athens: University of Georgia Press, 1970.

Kniffen, Fred B.; Hiram F. Gregory; and George A. Stokes. *The Historic Indian Tribes of Louisiana, from 1542 to the Present*. Baton Rouge: Louisiana State University Press, 1987.

Lankford, George E. and W. K. McNeil. *Native American Legends: Southeastern Legends—Tales from the Natchez, Caddo, Biloxi, Chickasaw, and Other Nations*. American Folklore Series. Little Rock: August House, 1987

Lazenby, Mary Elinor. *Catawba Frontier, 1775–1781: Memories of Pensioners*. Washington: Privately printed, 1950.

Merrell, James H. *The Catawbas*. New York: Chelsea House, ca.1989.

Rountree, Helen C. *Pocahontas's People: The Powhatan Indians of Virginia through Four Centuries*. Norman: University of Oklahoma Press, 1990.

———. *The Powhatan Indians of Virginia: Their Traditional Culture*. Norman: University of Oklahoma Press, 1989.

Scaife, H. Lewis. *Catawba Indians of South Carolina: History and Condition of the Catawba Indians of South Carolina*. Washington: Government Printing Office, 1930.

Speck, Frank Gouldsmith. *Catawba Texts*. 1934. Reprint, New York: AMS Press, 1969.

Swanton, John R. *A Structural and Lexical Comparison of the Tunica, Chitimacha, and Atakapa Languages*. 1919. Reprint, St. Clair Shores, Mich.: Scholarly Press, 1976.

———. *Source Material on the History and Ethnology of the Caddo Indians*. 1942. Reprint, Norman: University of Oklahoma Press, 1996.

INDEX

CPSIA information
Printed in the USA
BVOW02s1405171
379706BV00